Annotated Teacher's Edition

. . . a resource of student activities
to accompany the
Write Source 2000 and
All Write handbooks

Level 8

WRITE SOURCE®

GREAT SOURCE EDUCATION GROUP
a Houghton Mifflin Company
Wilmington, Massachusetts

A Few Words About the *Write Source 2000 SkillsBook: Level 8*

Before you begin . . .

The *SkillsBook* provides you with opportunities to practice the editing and proofreading skills presented in the *Write Source 2000* and *All Write* handbooks. The handbooks contain guidelines, examples, and models to help you complete your work in the *SkillsBook*.

Each *SkillsBook* activity includes a brief introduction to the topic and examples illustrating how to complete that activity. You will be directed to the page numbers in the handbook for additional information and examples. The "Proofreading Activities" focus on punctuation and the mechanics of writing. The "Sentence Activities" provide practice in sentence combining and in correcting common sentence problems. The "Language Activities" highlight each of the eight parts of speech.

The Next Step

Most activities include a **Next Step** at the end of the exercise. The purpose of the Next Step is to provide ideas for follow-up work that will help you apply what you have learned to your own writing.

Important Note: If you are using this *SkillsBook* with the *All Write* handbook, refer to the handbook numbers at the bottom of each page. The numbers are printed in color.

Authors: Pat Sebranek and Dave Kemper

Printed in the United States of America

International Standard Book Number: 978-0-669-46778-9 (student edition)

5 6 7 8 9 10 -POO- 05 04 03 02

International Standard Book Number: 978-0-669-46781-9 (teacher's edition)

6 7 8 9 10 -POO- 10 09 08 07

Table of Contents

Proofreading Activities

Sentence Activities

Sentence Basics

Sentence Combining

Sentence Problems

Sentence Variety

Language Activities

Nouns

Pronouns

Verbs

Adjectives

Adverbs

Prepositions

Interjections

Conjunctions

Parts of Speech

Proofreading Activities

Every activity in this section includes sentences that need to be checked for punctuation, mechanics, or correct word choices. Most of the activities also include helpful handbook references. In addition, the **Next Step** activities encourage follow-up practice of certain skills.

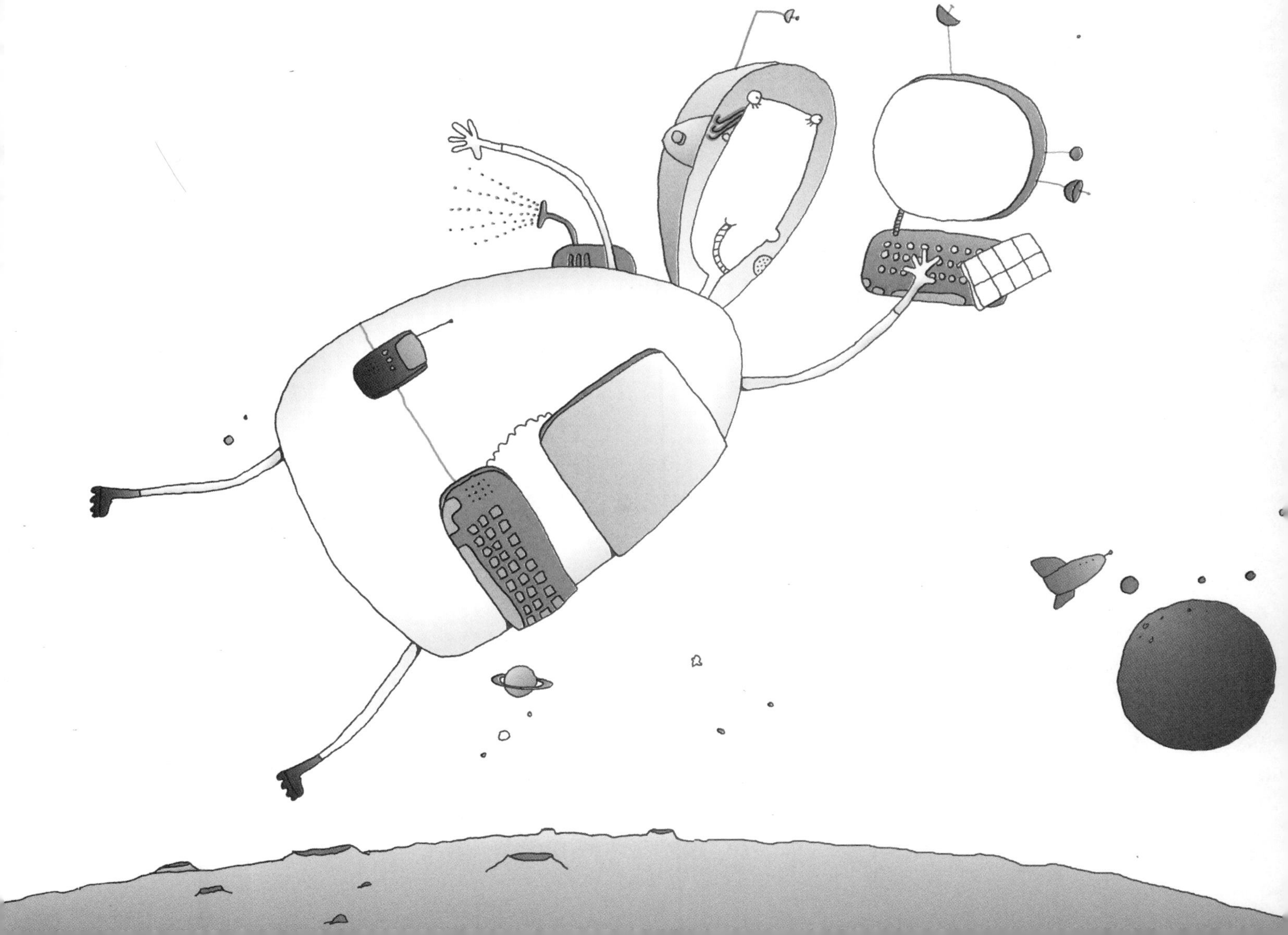

End Punctuation

Stop! Look? Listen. **End punctuation** is like a traffic cop. It controls the movement of your writing, telling the reader "Stop here!" It directs the reader to "ask a question," to "show emphasis," to "state a fact."

End punctuation marks—*periods, exclamation points, question marks*—make the reader put on his or her brakes at the end of each complete thought. (For more information about end punctuation and capitalization turn to 387.1, 398.1-398.2, 398.4, and 405.1 in your *Write Source 2000* handbook.)

Directions **Place periods, question marks, and exclamation points where they are needed in the following narrative. Also supply the necessary capital letters. The first paragraph has been done for you.**

I had applied for a position on the yearbook staff during the first week of school what a thrill to find out I made it was I going to be able to do a good job I would find out on group-picture day

my friends and I were excited that it was finally group-picture day Gabriella, Kim, and I were responsible for making sure that everybody who was in a group got his or her picture taken what a difficult job how could we be sure that everybody would be in the right place at the right time were we up to this task we were about to find out

we decided that the teachers themselves should make sure that all of their activity members were at the right place at the right time for the pictures we told the teachers to check off the students' names as they arrived for their appointments we provided the checklists what a great idea I'd like to take credit for the checklists unfortunately, I can't it was Kim's brainstorm

we also made sure that announcements were made at regular intervals so students were constantly reminded of the picture schedule ahead of time one announcement read, "Please have students from student council report to the multipurpose room" the announcements were my responsibility

we scheduled all groups during the morning periods when no students had gym would you want your picture taken in a "geeky" gym suit what a fantastic system do it right, and it will go right

i'm happy that nothing went wrong as a matter of fact, everything went very well the only thing the students had to do to get their picture in the yearbook was listen for the announcements of their activities and get checked off by their advisers of course, they also had to smile and say, "cheeeeeese"

Next Step Write a journal entry about an experience in your life that first worried you but, when it finally arrived, turned out to be no problem at all. Organize your thoughts in chronological order and try to use transition words (*next, finally,* etc.). Don't forget to "spice up" your writing with all four of the different types of sentences: *commands, statements, exclamations,* and *questions.*

Comma Rules

The punctuation mark that has the most uses (and probably causes the most confusion) is the comma. You will want to become familiar with the comma rules in your handbook. (Turn to 389.1-392.2 in *Write Source 2000.*)

Directions **Place commas correctly in each sample sentence. Then explain the rule that applies to that use of commas.**

1. I love to spend time at amusement parks, movies, and concerts.

   Rule: Commas are used between words, phrases, or clauses in a series.

2. There were 4 0,0 0 0 people at the last concert I attended.

   Rule: Commas are used to distinguish hundreds, thousands, millions, and so on, in numbers.

3. We ordered tickets from Ticketmaster, 4004 West Main Street, Chicago, Illinois 60010. The tickets will arrive by May 5, 1999.

   Rule: Commas are used in addresses and dates to make them clearer.

4. "Yes," said Dad, "you can take some friends to the concert."

   Rule: Commas are used to set off the exact words of the speaker from the rest of the sentence.

5. No, we don't want to sit in the back rows of the stadium.

   Rule: Commas are used to separate an interjection or a weak exclamation from the rest of the sentence.

6. The front row, if you asked me, would be the best place to sit.

Rule: Commas are used to set off an interruption of the main thought of a sentence.

7. We were going to take the van, but it wouldn't start.

Rule: A comma may be used between two independent clauses that are joined by a coordinating conjunction.

8. Tickets came addressed to Leroy Adams, D.D.S., and Peter Kendall, Ph.D.

Rule: Commas are used to enclose a title, a name, or initials that follow a person's last name.

9. We beamed with joy as we held the expensive, long-awaited tickets.

Rule: Commas are used to separate two or more adjectives that equally modify the same noun.

10. After many months passed, the day of the concert arrived. During that seemingly endless wait, another act had been added to the show.

Rule: A comma should separate an adverb clause or long modifying phrase from the independent clause that follows it.

11. Outdoor concerts aren't my favorite, but they are fun in good weather.

Rule: A comma may be used between two independent clauses that are joined by a coordinating conjunction.

12. My dad, an expert concertgoer, was a big help in our planning.

Rule: Commas should separate an explanatory phrase (or a nonrestrictive appositive) from the rest of the sentence.

Commas in a Series

Commas are needed to separate words, phrases, or clauses in a series. A series must always contain at least three items. (Turn to 389.1 in your *Write Source 2000* handbook for more information.)

EXAMPLE

To Separate Items in a Series:
A good baseball player must be able to hit, run, and field.

Directions **Insert commas where needed to separate items in a series in the sentences below. The first sentence has been done for you.**

1. Hitting a ball, running the bases, and fielding a position demand different skills.
2. Most good hitters have great eyesight, quick reflexes, and strong wrists.
3. Knowing the pitcher's moves, taking the longest possible lead, and getting the jump on the catcher are essentials for a good base runner.
4. Fielding any position well requires having a strong throwing arm, a knowledge of opposing hitters, and an ability to move quickly in any direction.
5. Regular practice, intense concentration, and good coaching are all important factors in a player's development.
6. Players must ignore noisy fans, bad calls by umpires, and insults from the opposing players' bench.
7. Ignoring distractions, staying cool, and keeping focused are often as important as hitting, running, or fielding.

8. Enjoying the company of team members, being out in the fresh air, and getting some exercise are all benefits of playing baseball.

9. Do some warm-up exercises, grab your glove, and go play ball.

10. Individual sports like tennis, golf, and archery also have their rewards.

11. Golf can sometimes be a frustrating, exasperating, and challenging game.

12. Crooked drives, erratic putts, and topped balls can plague even the most enthusiastic golfer.

13. Sand traps, water hazards, and rough greens provide added difficulties.

14. Despite sliced drives, lost balls, and terrible scores, many enjoy nothing more than a good round of golf.

Next Step Items in a series should be parallel. A well-constructed series in which each item is of the same type will make your writing more balanced and will lead to smoother reading. On your own paper, write five sentences. Use a parallel series of items in each sentence. Vary your series to include words, phrases, and clauses.

Commas Between Independent Clauses

A comma should be used with a coordinate conjunction between two independent clauses in a compound sentence. Coordinate conjunctions include words such as these: *but, or, nor, and, for, so,* and *yet.* Combining independent clauses to form compound sentences can add variety to your writing. (See 391.1 in your *Write Source 2000* handbook.) ***Note:*** Do not confuse a simple sentence containing a compound verb with a compound sentence.

EXAMPLES

Dalton eats too much, *but* he blames his weight on genetics.
(The comma and conjunction *but* are used to connect the two independent clauses in this compound sentence.)

Dalton eats too much and blames his weight on genetics.
(In this sentence *eats* and *blames* form the compound verb of a simple sentence.)

Directions **Study the sentences below. If the sentence contains two independent clauses, add a comma before the conjunction. The first one has been done for you.**

1. Dalton always smiles after losing a game, but he still hates losing.
2. Dalton smiles but still hates losing.
3. It was too rainy to go in-line skating, so we watched a video.
4. Jon wanted to shoot baskets with his dad, but he had promised to go biking with his brother.
5. Marcie usually loses at Scrabble but always wants to play the game.
6. She plays, yet she never improves at Scrabble.
7. Marcie bought a new dictionary, and she plans to study it every day.
8. After school, Zeke e-mailed three friends and then delivered papers.

All Write p. 316

Commas with Equal Adjectives

Two or more adjectives that equally modify the same noun should be separated with commas. There are two simple "equality" tests. Try switching the order of the adjectives. If the meaning of the sentence remains clear, the adjectives are equal. You can also insert "and" between the adjectives. If the sentence makes sense and reads well, you can use a comma. Try both tests on the sentence below. (Turn to section 391.3 in your *Write Source 2000* handbook for more information.)

EXAMPLE

Decent, good-hearted **people sometimes avoid homeless individuals.**
(Both tests work for this sentence, so the adjectives are equal and require a comma.)

Directions **Insert commas between equal adjectives where needed. *Note:* Do not place a comma after the last adjective.**

1. Healthy-looking, well-dressed pedestrians often look away when they come in contact with ragged, penniless street people.
2. What those fresh-scrubbed, well-groomed people don't realize is that with a bit of bad luck they also might be begging on the corner.
3. Many of those unwashed, undernourished homeless people may have held high-paying management jobs in the city.
4. Perhaps they owned spacious, landscaped homes in the suburbs and drove sleek, shiny cars.
5. Any confident, successful person today could still face failure tomorrow.
6. Be careful before judging those who eat in soup kitchens and sleep on dangerous, garbage-laden curbsides.

Next Step For each of the equal adjectives you found in the sentences above, substitute your own adjective.

Commas to Set Off Introductory Clauses and Phrases

A comma is used to separate an **introductory adverb clause** or a **long introductory phrase** from the independent clause that follows it. You should note, however, that no comma is required when a short introductory phrase begins the sentence or when the adverb clause follows the main clause. (Study the examples below and section 391.2 in your *Write Source 2000* handbook to help clarify these exceptions.)

EXAMPLES

In spring **dairy farmers are busy planting crops.**
(No comma is required after "spring" because the introductory phrase is short.)

After spring planting is done, **there is still plenty to do.**
(A comma sets off the introductory adverb clause.)

There is still plenty to do ***after spring planting is done.***
(No comma is required because the adverb clause follows the main clause.)

Directions **Read the sentences below carefully and insert commas where they are needed. There are three sentences that do not require commas. The first one has been done for you.**

1. Regardless of the season or day of the week, dairy farmers have plenty to do to keep them busy.
2. Because cows do not observe holidays, they must be milked every day.
3. If a farmer is to succeed, he or she must follow nature's schedule.
4. With nature running the show, the farmer has very little choice.
5. Modern equipment helps the farmer because it cuts out some of the backbreaking labor.

All Write p. 316

6. Over the next decade or two, a farmer's day will probably get shorter as equipment increases his or her productivity.

7. Be it hail, wind, or drought, farmers are at the mercy of the weather.

8. Rain is welcome during the summer although it can be a problem at harvesttime.

9. In addition to late-season rains, an early frost can also be damaging to a crop.

10. Although 12 hours is an average day, farmers work longer during harvest.

11. Since harvesting is so important, every working day is crucial.

12. As my neighbor John Williams once told me, nature is the world's toughest boss.

13. John often complains about farming even though he loves his life on the farm.

14. For the past fifty years, John has been a very good friend.

Next Step Take some time to review information on dependent and independent clauses in your *Write Source 2000* handbook. Looking at sections 436.3-438.2 on clauses, phrases, and types of sentences should be helpful. Then go back over this exercise and underline the independent clause within each sentence.

All Write pp. 370-372

Commas with Nonrestrictive Clauses

Commas are used to set off nonrestrictive clauses from the rest of a sentence. **Nonrestrictive clauses** are clauses that may be removed from a sentence without changing the basic meaning of the sentence. Study the examples below. (Turn to 392.2 in your *Write Source 2000* for more about this use of commas.)

EXAMPLES

Nonrestrictive Clause:

Roger, who has passed all his finals, will graduate in June.
(The clause *who has passed all his finals* adds information to the sentence but is not necessary to make the basic meaning clear.)

Restrictive Clause:

Students who have passed all their finals will graduate in June.
(The clause *who have passed all their finals* is needed to make clear which students are eligible to graduate. It restricts the meaning of the sentence, so no commas are required.) ***Note:*** Phrases may also be restrictive.

Directions

Place commas around nonrestrictive clauses in the following sentences. (Place *no* commas around restrictive clauses.) The first one has been done for you.

1. The American writer Ernest Hemingway was fond of Spain, which he visited many times.

2. Hemingway, who traveled a great deal, also spent time in France, Africa, and Cuba.

3. Hemingway's style, which influenced thousands of writers, appeared simple and effortless.

4. Hemingway, who was a perfectionist, would often write less than 500 words a day.

5. New York's Strand Bookstore, which is the largest used-book store in the country, contains more than six miles of books.

6. Robert Frost, who became America's best-known poet, first gained fame in England.

7. The old book that Julie found was worth more than fifty dollars.

8. Soccer, which has long been a favorite sport in Europe and South America, is now becoming popular in the United States.

9. Babe Ruth, who became baseball's greatest hitter, began his career as a pitcher.

10. My little brother won't go back to the ballpark where he once got lost.

Directions **Write three correctly punctuated sentences containing nonrestrictive clauses.**

1. ____

____

2. ____

____

3. ____

____

Next Step Exchange your sentences with a classmate. Check each other's sentences to see if they are correct. If there is any doubt about a particular sentence, turn to 392.2 in your *Write Source 2000* handbook and make corrections.

Commas in Dialogue, Interruptions, and Interjections

In **dialogue,** commas are used to set off the exact words of the speaker from the rest of the sentence. Here is one example: "Don't mix dialogue and narrative," said the teacher, "but separate them with commas and quotation marks."

Brief shifts of focus in a sentence are also marked by commas. Shifting reflects natural breaks or pauses you might take when reading a passage aloud. Shifting might be caused by **interruptions, nouns of direct address,** or **interjections.** Notice the shifting in this sentence: "Yes, George, you did, as a matter of fact, receive the highest grade on the Mr. Wizard genius exam." (See the examples below and sections 390.1-390.4 in your *Write Source 2000* handbook for more information.)

EXAMPLES

The boss said, "You may have a raise."
(A comma sets off the speaker's exact words from the rest of the sentence.)

The raise, *however,* was small.
(*However* is set off from the rest of the sentence because it interrupts the flow of the sentence and can be omitted without changing the basic meaning of the sentence.)

***"Jack,* did you know about the raise?" asked André.**
(The person directly addressed—being spoken to—is set off with a comma.)

***"Yes,* I did."**
(Interjections like *yes* and mild exclamations are separated from the remainder of the sentence by a comma.)

Directions **Place commas where needed in the sentences below. The first one has been done for you.**

"André, you know that assignment is due tomorrow," scolded Mary. André said, "Why do you think I'm hurrying?" He, as a matter of fact, didn't really seem to be in a big rush.

All Write pp. 314 and 315

He had, for example, just used 20 minutes to type a single paragraph.

"Gosh," Mary commented, "if that's fast, I'd hate to see slow."

"Mary, haven't you ever heard that haste makes waste?" asked André.

"Yes, but I've also heard that late assignments get bad grades," replied Mary.

"Mary, I've never been late with an assignment yet, and I don't intend to start now," André stated in his own defense.

"Well, there's a first time for everything, so if I were you, I'd hurry just a little," warned Mary.

"As a matter of fact, I am thinking of ways to work faster," André said slowly.

"Sure you are, Andre," said Mary.

"Say, Mary, I could work faster if I ate something," hinted André.

"Actually, a snack is not a bad idea. I'll make some popcorn. You start typing," replied Mary.

"Pizza sounds even better," André said, grinning, as his fingers started to fly across the keyboard.

"Whoa, I think we finally found the solution to your typing block," laughed Mary.

Next Step Using your own paper, write two sentences for each of the four types of commas covered in this exercise. Share your sentences with a classmate and check each other's punctuation.

Comma Review 1

Here's a chance for you to practice two important uses of commas. Review the examples below before you begin your work. (Also turn to 392.1 in *Write Source 2000* for more examples.)

EXAMPLES

A comma is used to set off a nonrestrictive appositive:
His essay, *a look at using gun detectors in schools,* was thought-provoking.
(The appositive is a phrase, a phrase not needed for the sentence to be clear.)

John gave his last M&M to his only brother, *Scott.*
(The appositive is a word, a word not needed in the sentence.)

A comma is not used to set off a restrictive appositive:
I had borrowed one dollar from my friend *Ben.*
(*Ben* is a restrictive appositive because the reader would not know which friend is being referred to if the specific name were not used; *Ben* is needed for the sentence to be clear.)

Directions **Underline the appositives in the sentences below. Add commas where necessary.**

1. I've got six brothers but only one sister Jennie.
2. She has three pets a hamster and two goldfish.
3. Her goldfish Stella chases the other one around the tank.
4. The smaller fish Sid tries to hide in the plants.
5. Jennie thinks she might have to add something else maybe another fish to the tank.
6. My brother Bill had fish when he was younger, but he never had this problem.
7. The theory that big fish always eat little fish appears to be true.
8. Or maybe big fish like Stella just need more exercise.

All Write p. 318

Comma Review 2

Here's a chance for you to practice two more uses of commas. Review the examples below before you begin your work. (Also turn to 392.2 in *Write Source 2000* for more examples.)

EXAMPLES

A comma is used to set off a nonrestrictive clause:

The report, which was thoroughly researched, received an A+.

(The clause *which was thoroughly researched* is purely descriptive and could be eliminated without changing the meaning of the sentence. Commas are required.)

A comma is not used to set off a restrictive clause:

The report that the police officer made convinced us to obey the curfew.

(The clause *that the police officer made* is necessary to the meaning of the sentence.)

Note: When you are trying to decide whether to start your clause with *which* or with *that,* use *which* for nonrestrictive clauses and *that* for restrictive.

Directions **Underline the restrictive clauses and the nonrestrictive clauses in the sentences below. Add commas where necessary.**

1. My cousin's bus is one of the new ones that run on natural gas.
2. My bus which is one of the old yellow ones runs on smelly diesel fuel.
3. When my driver is late which is unusual she says it's because she doesn't have enough passengers.
4. Traffic is a problem because there are too many people who are driving their own cars instead of taking buses.
5. Alex who has a chronic cough says that air pollution is a bad problem in our city.
6. There would be less traffic and less pollution if more people who now ride alone in their cars rode buses.
7. Alex's method of getting to school which is walking doesn't pollute.

Punctuating Dialogue

Having a conversation is simple. Someone says something. Someone else responds, and a conversation is under way. Written conversations are a little more difficult. They need to be correctly punctuated to make sense. (Study the examples below; then turn to 390.1 and 400.1 in your *Write Source 2000* handbook for help.)

EXAMPLES

"I'm tired," said Mark. "This broken arm is wearing me out."
(A period comes after *Mark* because that's the end of a complete sentence.)

"Oh yeah," joked Ken, "you need to give your arm a rest."
(A comma comes after *Ken* because what follows completes the sentence.)

"Is that the best broken-arm joke you can think of?" Mark asked.
(The question mark is placed inside the quotation marks because the quotation is the question.)

Directions

Punctuate the following sentences with quotation marks, commas, and end marks. The first one has been done for you. (*Note:* See how correct punctuation makes the dialogue easier to follow.)

Jessie, I think you dropped your pen warned Jon Jessie started searching for her pen

Have you done the English homework asked Jessie It's really long

No replied Jon I haven't read it yet I planned to read it in the library this afternoon.

Don't forget said Jessie you also have to write an essay.

It's a good thing you reminded me because I had forgotten all about the essay Jon said.

All Write pp. 314 and 324

I'll be thinking about you slaving away while I'm enjoying the movie gloated Jessie

What are you going to see asked Jon

I'm going to see *Titanic* Jessie responded

Yeah I hear the special effects in *Titanic* are awesome Jon said I'm really not into disaster films that much

I'm not usually either said Jessie but I have a special interest in this one My great-grandparents were supposed to have been on that ship

Wow Jon said That's a case where missing the boat was a good thing

Well I just hope you don't miss the boat with that English assignment Jessie said as she sailed out the door

Next Step Here's your chance to get a little creative with dialogue. Make up a dialogue between two fictional persons. Don't explain who the characters are or what the situation is about. Rather, let the characters develop naturally during the conversation. Continue the dialogue until you come to a natural stopping point. Make sure to punctuate your sentences correctly.

Apostrophes 1

The possessive of singular nouns is usually formed by adding an apostrophe and an *s* as in the examples below. (Turn to 402.4-403.4 in your *Write Source 2000* handbook for more information.)

EXAMPLES

To Form Singular Possessives:

Mr. Brown's assignment

(For most nouns, add an apostrophe and an *s.*)

the Rio Lobos' depth *or* the Rio Lobos's depth

(For singular, multisyllable nouns ending with an *s* or a *z* sound, add an apostrophe only or an apostrophe and an *s.*)

the moss's color

(For one-syllable nouns ending in *s,* add an apostrophe and an *s.*)

Directions **Write the correct singular possessive form above each underlined singular noun in the following sentences. The first sentence has been done for you.**

John's
1. Did John team win the soccer tournament?

girl's
2. The girl dress was too formal for the party.

somebody else's
3. It was somebody else loss, not mine.

boss's
4. The boss salary was much larger than mine.

sister-in-law's
5. My sister-in-law car was a bright red convertible.

student's
6. They found the student book in the back of the classroom.

Massachusetts' or Massachusetts's
7. Massachusetts population is large compared to its small size.

brother's
8. The messy room was my brother.

Ms. Jenks's
9. Your guess is as good as Ms. Jenks guess.

pass's
10. The mountain pass elevation was 10,500 feet.

Directions **Write the correct possessive form above each underlined singular noun in the following sentences. The first one has been done for you.**

Kiss's
1. I thought Kiss last album was a disappointment.

Someone else's
2. Someone else opinion may be different from mine.

brother-in-law's
3. My brother-in-law opinion sometimes differs from mine.

everyone's
4. In fact, his opinion seems different from almost everyone.

Jane's
5. Alex, Paul, and Jane team won the championship.

St. Louis' or St. Louis's
6. St. Louis main tourist attraction is the Gateway Arch.

jazz's
7. What is jazz fascination?

Anyone's
8. Anyone ticket will get you into the concert on the green.

Yesterday's
9. What wit said, "Yesterday news is good for wrapping fish"?

Tess's
10. Tess final-exam grade was higher than mine.

Texas' or Texas's
11. Did Texas population increase by more than a million in the last decade?

room's
12. The room appearance could best be described as chaotic.

day's day's
13. Bill always gives a day work for a day pay.

Bob's
14. Bob and Matt's boats are tied at the dock.

mother-in-law's
15. John always appreciates his mother-in-law humor.

Next Step On your own paper, write the possessive form for each of the words listed below.

1. somebody *somebody's*
2. gas *gas's*
3. anyone *anyone's*
4. Dallas *Dallas' or Dallas's*
5. Max *Max's*
6. month *month's*
7. everyone *everyone's*
8. father-in-law *father-in-law's*

Apostrophes 2

An apostrophe is used to show that letters have been left out of words (don't), to show possession (Garfield's dinner), and to indicate time or amount (a day's work, a dollar's worth). (Read the example below; then turn to 402.1-403.4 in your *Write Source 2000* handbook for more information about apostrophes before you complete the following sentences.)

EXAMPLE

***"Didn't* your *sister's* puppy chew up *yesterday's* homework, Homer?"**

(In the word *Didn't* the apostrophe shows that the letter *o* has been left out; in *sister's* the apostrophe shows possession for the singular noun *sister;* in *yesterday's* the apostrophe indicates time.)

Directions **Add apostrophes to the following sentences. The first sentence has been done for you.**

1. "Ill get to tomorrows assignments after this TV show," I called.
2. Moms answer was, "No you wont. Youll work on them right now."
3. Mr. Basss homework wasnt too hard. It was the algebra I couldnt face.
4. Besides that, when the seasons new shows were on, it was hard to do work.
5. "Cant I take a break, Mom?" I pleaded as though my brains well-being was at stake.
6. "Youve been on break!" was my moms reply.
7. I shouldve finished my homework in study hall, but instead I helped Mr. Anderson with his bulletin board entitled "The Class of '99 in the Workplace."

8. Im learning that when students homework isnt done, it comes back to haunt them, so I started to work.

9. Whats going to be first, math problems or history?

10. What Id thought would be an hours worth of math, I completed in 15 minutes.

11. Historys next, I thought, and started without a moments delay.

12. Reading about wars makes a person appreciate soldiers sacrifices.

13. Soon I forgot Id been overloaded with three teachers assignments.

14. The evenings fears of bad grades in my classes vanished in the next 30 minutes, and the next days homework was completed.

15. My advice: Get tomorrows homework done today, or itll become tomorrows nightmare!

Next Step Review the rules for possessives in your handbook and then add apostrophes as needed in the following phrases:

- ❑ Fuddle, Muddle, and Bamboozles magic act
- ❑ Leonardos, Raphaels, and Michelangelos pizzas
- ❑ my brother-in-laws yo-yo
- ❑ their sisters-in-laws roller skates
- ❑ everybodys pet rock
- ❑ yesterdays fads

Apostrophes 3

The plural possessive of nouns ending in *s* is usually formed by adding an apostrophe after the *s.* Plural nouns not ending in *s* usually require an apostrophe and an *s.* (Turn to 402.5 and 403.4 in your *Write Source 2000* handbook for rules governing shared possession and the possessive of a compound noun.)

Directions **Write the possessive form of each plural noun below in the space provided below. The first one has been done for you.**

women's **1.** The women order for concert tickets was made in person.

parents' **2.** The boys, girls, and parents applause shook the rafters.

bosses' **3.** The bosses rules were strict.

brothers-in-law's **4.** The brothers-in-laws cars were identical.

toys' **5.** The toys storage box was broken.

Joneses' **6.** The Joneses family tree went back to the Civil War.

months' **7.** Two months worth of mail had collected on the porch.

girls' **8.** The girls opinions were extremely divided.

boys' **9.** The boys teams all won their games.

men's **10.** Who designed the mens uniforms?

bosses' **11.** The bosses offices are upstairs.

players' **12.** The players meals will be served in the gym.

Directions In the space provided, write the correct plural possessive form of the nouns listed. Add a word or two to complete the phrase. The first one has been done for you.

1. the girl — *the girls' project*
2. the dog — *the dogs' favorite food*
3. the child — *the children's swing set*
4. the boss — *the bosses' orders*
5. the man — *the men's volleyball team*
6. the team — *the teams' leading scorers*
7. the herd — *the herds' pasture*
8. the ex-president — *the ex-presidents' duties*
9. the pilgrim — *the pilgrims' ship*
10. the boy — *the boys' school*

Directions On the lines below, write three sentences containing plural possessives. Use a noun ending in *s,* a noun not ending in *s,* and a plural compound noun. (An example of a plural compound noun is "brothers-in-law.") Do not use nouns listed in this exercise.

1. ______________________________

____

2. ______________________________

____

3. ______________________________

____

Other Forms of Punctuation

As the thoughts you express in writing become more complex, punctuation marks become more important. Some of the most useful punctuation marks are *semicolons [;], colons [:], dashes [—], parentheses [( )],* and *hyphens [-].* (Turn to 393.1-397.3 in your *Write Source 2000* handbook for information about these special forms of punctuation.)

Directions **Using the punctuation rules in your handbook, place marks correctly in each sample sentence. Then explain the rule that applies to the punctuation mark you've used. The first one has been done for you.**

1. We raised money for our outdoor education program by selling pizzas and sausages; delivery day is today.

Rule: A semicolon is used to join two independent clauses when the clauses are not already connected with a coordinate conjunction.

2. To earn money, we sold the following: cheese pizzas, sausage pizzas, pepperoni pizzas, cutters, and sausages.

Rule: A colon is used to introduce a list.

3. The pizza order forms — (or) (I hope I added my totals up correctly — (or)) were handed in to Mr. Pennington.

Rule: A dash can show a sudden break in a sentence.
Or . . . Parentheses are used around words that add extra information.

4. After delivering hundreds of pizzas, I knew I soon wanted to become an ex-salesperson.

Rule: A hyphen is used to form new words beginning with the prefixes all, self, ex, great, etc.

— (or) (

5. The pizza order forms included information addresses, phone numbers,

— (or))

prices, customer totals that made the deliveries easy.

Rule: Parentheses are used around words that add extra information to a sentence. Or . . . A dash can show a sudden break in a sentence.

Directions **Punctuate the following sentences correctly by adding the necessary colons, semicolons, dashes, parentheses, and hyphens. The first one has been done for you.**

1. The truck pulled up with our 299 cases of pizzas; we all jumped to our stations.

2. We needed ten students to process the delivery system and five to give the parents some valuable information — where to park. *(for emphasis)* — (A colon may also be used.)

3. Each step of the system (sign-in, pickup, loading, and carryout) had to run like clockwork. *(added information)*

4. The driver had separated all of the items: cheese pizzas, sausage pizzas, pepperoni pizzas, pizza cutters, and sausages.

5. Safety is one thing that is very important — actually vital — in the car-loading station. *(sudden break)*

6. Mr. Pennington inspected the whole operation, but we all worked to make it an accident-free day. *(creating a new word)*

7. The sale was a success; we had handled 145 orders and 3,578 pizzas!

8. Mr. Pennington was happy. “I want you to know that we’ve earned about four — no, make that five — thousand dollars!”

Semicolons

A semicolon sometimes acts like a period and sometimes acts like a comma. For information about semicolons, turn to 393.1-393.4 in your *Write Source 2000* handbook.

EXAMPLES

To Join Two Independent Clauses:
I have a signed Batman comic; it is the most valuable book I own.

To Join Two Independent Clauses Connected by a Conjunctive Adverb:
My karate instructor was tough; however, he never got upset.
(Conjunctive adverbs include *also, as a result, besides, for example, furthermore, however, in addition, instead, meanwhile, moreover, nevertheless, similarly, then, therefore, thus.*)

To Separate Groups of Words or Phrases That Already Contain Commas:
My favorite foods are pizza with pepperoni, peppers, and mushrooms; peanut butter and jelly sandwiches; and liver and onions.

Directions **Place semicolons where appropriate in the following sentences. The first sentence has been done for you.**

1. John decided to go to a movie; he wanted to see *Deep Impact.*
2. Afterward, he said he didn't care for the film; he said he is getting tired of "disaster" movies.
3. Victor likes most films; nevertheless, he still refuses to see *Titanic.*
4. He won't go to war movies; he classifies them as "disaster" films.
5. Victor thinks there are enough real disasters around; he doesn't need them magnified on a wide screen with Dolby surround-sound.
6. Victor may be right; however, I was impressed by *Titanic* and loved being scared by *Deep Impact.*

7. I enjoy all kinds of movies; therefore, I don't plan to change my movie-going habits.

8. My favorite movies are *The Godfather, Part II;* *Star Trek, The Next Generation;* and *Titanic.*

9. I hate to get to the movies late; I want to see the previews.

10. I don't like to eat when I'm watching movies; besides, the food at the theater is so expensive.

11. People at the theater are sometimes rude; it can make the whole experience unpleasant.

12. Some people talk during the feature, get up to get food, go to the bathroom, or just change seats; and once someone fell asleep behind me and started snoring.

13. New theaters with stadium-style seating are nice; short people ought to especially like them.

14. I really like discount theaters; you can get a ticket and a big tub of popcorn for the same price as a ticket at a regular theater.

15. Sometimes I go to the discount theater even if I could rent the same movie at a video store; it's just more fun watching a movie on a big screen.

Next Step Now it's your turn to try the three different uses for the semicolon. Write a sentence of your own for each semicolon use covered in this exercise.

Colons

A colon may be used to introduce a list or an important point. It can also set off a word or phrase from the rest of the sentence for emphasis. A colon follows the salutation of a business letter and comes between numbers that show time. (Turn to 394.1-394.5 in your *Write Source 2000* handbook for additional information about colons.)

EXAMPLES

Dear Mr. Valenza:
(The colon follows the salutation of a business letter.)

Musician Wanda Landowska made this statement: "I never practice; I always play."
(The colon is used to formally introduce the quotation.)

Most burglaries take place between 1:00 a.m. and 4:00 a.m.
(The colon is used between numbers showing time.)

A good student does the following: reads, writes, and remembers.
(The colon introduces a list.)

The police were missing one important piece of information: a motive.
(The colon sets off the phrase *a motive* for emphasis.)

Directions **Place colons where they are needed in the following sentences. The first two sentences have been done for you.**

1. There was one problem with the 7:00 a.m. class: the time of day.
2. Dad's sports rules were the following: play hard, play fair, and play often.
3. John gave us some good advice for losing weight: eat less.
4. He also told us to avoid the following: eating between meals, eating before going to bed, and eating foods that are mostly sugar or salt.

5. The library doors were locked at exactly 5:00 p.m.

6. Lucas has three major dislikes: whiners, bullies, and braggarts.

7. On the other hand, there was one thing he really liked: football.

8. The most involved people have the least input in one area: education.

9. Students are often the last to be heard after the following groups have had their say: politicians, parents, administrators, and educators.

10. Some follow this saying: "Children should be seen and not heard."

Directions **Rewrite the sentences below so that each sentence uses one or more colons. The first sentence has been done for you.**

1. Reading, sleeping, and eating are Aaron's favorite activities.

   Aaron's favorite activities are the following: reading, sleeping, and eating.

2. Chad was lost in the woods from ten in the morning until eleven at night.

   Chad was lost in the woods from 10:00 a.m. until 11:00 p.m.

3. His backpack broke and spilled energy bars, a water bottle, and his flashlight.

   His backpack broke and spilled its contents: energy bars, a water bottle, and his flashlight.

4. "It's always darkest before dawn" was my grandfather's favorite saying.

   This was my grandfather's favorite saying: "It's always darkest before dawn."

5. The one thing I liked about Uncle Bill was listening to his scary campfire stories.

   There was one thing I really liked about Uncle Bill: listening to his scary campfire stories.

Hyphens 1

Hyphens are used to divide words at the end of a line. They are also used between numbers in fractions, to avoid awkward spellings, and to join certain letters and words. (Turn to 396.1-397.3 in your *Write Source 2000* handbook for more about using hyphens.)

EXAMPLES

She won the race by six-tenths of a second.
(The hyphen is used between numbers in the fraction.)

She had to re-create her report after her soda spilled on it.
(The hyphen avoids confusion in the word *re-create.*)

The T-bar on the ski lift was broken.
(The hyphen joins a letter and a word.)

Directions **Divide the following words as they should be divided at the end of a line. If the example is already divided correctly, write *C* in the space; if the example is incorrect, write out the word and hyphenate it correctly. (For help, refer to 396.1 in your *Write Source 2000* handbook.) The first two have been done for you.**

1.	cau-ght	caught	**10.**	bro-ken	C
2.	es-cape	C	**11.**	par-agraph	para-graph
3.	hea-ven	heav-en	**12.**	taught	C
4.	does-n't	doesn't	**13.**	sud-den	C
5.	e-rased	erased	**14.**	num-ber	C
6.	hyp-hen	hy-phen	**15.**	cent-er	cen-ter
7.	div-ide	di-vide	**16.**	tour-ist	C
8.	fract-ion	frac-tion	**17.**	can-dy	candy
9.	re-fer	refer	**18.**	his-tory	C

Directions **Place hyphens as needed in the following sentences. The first sentence has been done for you.**

1. Yesterday my cousin turned twenty-one.
2. He moved the high-jump bar exactly one-quarter of an inch higher for a record-setting attempt.
3. My parents wouldn't let me see the R-rated movie.
4. The game was three-fourths over, and Bob hadn't missed a single three-point shot.
5. He came back from Chicago with a fashionably ragged pair of jeans and his usual start-of-winter cold.
6. We will have to re-cover the chair because it looks too worn to go with our new indoor-outdoor carpeting.
7. The standard photos come only in four-inch widths; enlargements come in 5-by-8-inch or 9-by-12-inch sizes.
8. The Kennedy-Nixon television debate is an important event in political history.
9. His self-conscious cousin was nervous about performing in the third-grade holiday pageant.
10. We need to recruit six 12-year-old girls for our volleyball team.

Next Step Create new words beginning with the prefixes *self, all,* and *great*. Write a sentence for each word.

Hyphens 2

Hyphens may be used to form compound words, single-thought adjectives, and new words using certain prefixes and suffixes. (See 396.2, 397.1, and 397.3 in *Write Source 2000* for additional examples of the uses of hyphens.)

EXAMPLES

I hit fast-forward to watch my favorite part of a movie.
(*Fast-forward* is a compound word.)

My collection of award-winning films includes 20 comedies.
(*Award-winning* is a single-thought adjective modifying *films.*)

***The Wild Bunch* is my all-time favorite western.**
(*All-time* is a new word formed by combining the prefix *all* with *time.*)

Directions **Read the sentences below and insert hyphens where necessary between compound words, single-thought adjectives, and new words formed by using prefixes and suffixes. The first one has been done for you.**

1. People probably should eat more fat-free foods.
2. Hard-to-understand instructions seem like they are written in Greek.
3. The heart-pounding ending left me breathless.
4. The "easy-to-follow" instructions for the new VCR confused me.
5. The new book of student-written poems was high on my must-read list.
6. The 12-year-old skating champion fell after trying the triple jump.
7. I stopped at a fast-food deli for lunch.
8. The one-run loss was becoming routine for the hard-luck baseball team.
9. It's time to replace my out-of-date printer with an ink-jet model.
10. The company halted in-house production of its magazine.

Dashes

You probably will not find many reasons to use dashes in your writing. Still, you should know when and how to use dashes. (Review the examples below and consult 395.1-395.3 in *Write Source 2000* for additional explanations and examples.) You should note that dashes are formed by two hyphens--without spacing before or after--in any typed work.

EXAMPLES

The 1998 New York Yankees were an amazing team—in fact, an astonishing team—during regular and postseason play.
(To indicate sudden breaks in sentences.)

After winning the American League championship, the team had a final goal—sweeping the World Series.
(To set off a word, a phrase, or a clause for emphasis.)

Oh no—not that—yes, I heard you, but I can't believe it.
(To show interrupted speech.)

Directions **In the sentences below, insert dashes where they are needed. The first one has been done for you.**

1. The 1998 Yankees had one aim and one aim only—winning.
2. I think the Yankees have proven—proven beyond a shadow of a doubt—that they have more overall talent than anyone else.
3. After 162 regular season games and 15 postseason games, the players had one thing in mind—a long vacation without any baseball.
4. Playing more than 170 games can be wearing—even on the most dedicated player.
5. Each Yankee player will receive something special—a World Series ring.

Next Step Using the sentences above as models, write your own five sentences about a favorite sports team. Include each of the three uses for a dash at least once.

All Write p. 322

Italics and Quotation Marks

When you've written a story or essay that contains a book title or a slang word or the title of a favorite TV show, you must decide whether to **italicize** that piece of information or put **quotation marks** around it. Titles of longer works—and the names of ships and aircraft—should be italicized. Articles, book chapters, and television episodes are enclosed in quotation marks.

Also, a word or phrase being used in a special way, or a word that is slang, is enclosed in quotation marks. (See 400.2-400.3 and 401.1-401.5 in your *Write Source 2000* handbook.)

Directions **Underline titles that should be in italics and insert quotation marks where needed. The first one has been done for you.**

1. Because of television spin-offs and films, the starship Enterprise's "continuing mission" seems destined to go on forever.
2. He's such a good player, the others say he's "bad."
3. Air Force One is the name of a plane and the title of a film.
4. I think "Stopping by Woods on a Snowy Evening" is one of Robert Frost's best poems.
5. My father's least favorite word is "bugged."
6. My mother reads the New York Times, Newsweek, and the Washington Post to keep up with current news.
7. My favorite song from Paul Simon's Graceland album is "You Can Call Me Al."

Next Step Think of several slang or special-use words that you and your friends would say. Now write a sentence or two using those words. Be sure to mark the punctuation correctly.

Punctuation Review 1

Directions **Proofread the paragraphs below. Draw a line through any mark of punctuation or capital letter that is used incorrectly. Add any needed punctuation or capital letters. The first two lines have been done for you.**

an octopus is a marine animal with eight arms called tentacles. It has a soft body large eyes and a strong jaw. The octopus uses its arms to catch clams crabs lobsters and other shellfish for food. It cuts up its food with its horny jaws, which come to a point like a birds beak. Because of octopuses scary appearance some people call them devilfish but octopuses rarely if ever attack people.

Most of the 50 different kinds of octopuses are actually about the size of a persons fist. There are larger ones however that measure 28 feet from the tip of one arm to the tip of another but even these octopuses are more likely to be eaten by humans than the other way around. Octopuses live chiefly in the China and Mediterranean Seas and many people in these regions eat octopus meat.

The octopus in almost every respect is a one of a kind creature it has no bones and no shell, but it does have a highly-developed brain an octopus also has three hearts. It swims by drawing water into it's body and then squeezing it out in bursts through a funnel shaped opening under it's head. The force of the water propels the octopus backward the octopus can also squirt out a black fluid, that forms a cloud around the animal, hiding it from its enemies.

Punctuation Review 2

Directions **Read the paragraphs below carefully. Draw a line through any errors in punctuation and capitalization. Add punctuation and capitalization as needed. The first few errors have been corrected for you.**

The Murders in the Rue Morgue a short story by Edgar Allan Poe is thought to be the first example of the detective story. Although Poe's character C. Auguste Dupin may have been the first fictional detective he is by no means the best-known that honor certainly falls to Sir Arthur Conan Doyle's immortal Sherlock Holmes Holmes who is known to millions of readers and viewers around the world first appeared in 1887. Doyle's books as well as numerous films and television shows feature Sherlock and his constant companion, Dr. Watson

The reasons for Holmes enduring popularity are themselves a bit of a mystery for in many ways Holmes was not a very likeable person. He was short tempered and he was unkind to other detectives, especially Police Inspector Lestrade of Scotland Yard.

Holmes's ever questioning mind and dislike for displays of emotion made him appear cold calculating and uncaring. He was an expert violin player and could play beautifully when he felt like it Holmes in fact was very moody. When he had nothing to occupy his mind he became bored and depressed. He would sit around for days making

All Write pp. 311-327

horrible squawks and screeches on the violin, which drove Dr. Watson nearly crazy.

holmes was not exactly a picture perfect roommate either. He left chemicals for his scientific experiments all over the place and he kept his smelly messy pipe tobacco in his old, bedroom slippers. He stuck his mail to the mantle with a penknife and he stashed his many book's and papers wherever it seemed convenient at the time.

Despite Holmes' cool personality and his weird personal habits Watson was genuinely fond of him and although he rarely showed it Holmes also cared deeply for his friend. When Doyle made it appear that Holmes had died while fighting with Dr. Moriarty Holmes' (or) Holmes's ~~Holme's~~ toughest opponent the reaction against Doyle was tremendous. People responded as though a longtime personal friend had died. real people seemed just as upset as the fictional Dr. Watson at the report of Holmes' death. After three years Watson and thousands of fans breathed a sigh of relief when Sir Arthur Conan Doyle brought Holmes back.

Next Step Once you go through this exercise finding as many errors as you can, you might want to check your answers with a classmate (if your teacher doesn't object). If you discover differences in your corrections, you then might want to discuss them and check in your handbook. Then make additional corrections as needed.

Capitalization and Abbreviations

Attention to detail means different things depending on the task, but the result will always be the same: a better party, a tastier pizza, and a finer piece of writing.

In this activity you will review a series of phrases or sentences to make sure that capital letters and abbreviations have properly been put in place. (Turn to 404.1-407.3 and 409.4-409.6 in your *Write Source 2000* handbook for more information on capitalization and abbreviations.)

Directions

Put a line through any word or letter below that is capitalized or abbreviated incorrectly. Correct each error. One way to do this would be to go through the list once and make the changes you're sure of. Then, for those that you question, review the rules in your handbook. The first sentence has been done for you. (*Note:* Do *not* abbreviate the names of states, countries, months, days, or units of measure in formal writing. Also do not use signs or symbols [%, &] in place of words.)

S M S G S

1. We are looking for a project for our springfield middle school global studies

F January

fair held in ~~jan~~.

M

2. How about a fiesta highlighting mexican culture?

W W

3. what a great idea for the middle of Winter!

M B s s

4. mr. brown, our Social Studies teacher, is asking each class to do its part.

O G S

5. our class, global studies 101, will bring the food.

Mr. B

6. ~~mister~~ brown says that other classes will be responsible for planning the

Wednesday

schedule of events by this ~~Wed~~.

S P T Association

7. Should we get parents involved from the springfield parent teacher ~~assoc~~.?

All Write pp. 328-332 and 335

8. Yes, we need a lot of help and maybe a few ~~$'s,~~ dollars too.

9. The fiesta will involve spanish music and festival customs from ~~Mex~~ Mexico.

10. mr. whitman, the gym teacher, will teach all of the Eighth Graders the mexican hat dance.

11. in the Art Classes, all of the students will make posters and wall decorations.

12. The springfield middle school band will perform special music for the fiesta.

13. the band director, mr. ames, has written an original fiesta song, and he tells us it's called "the old brown dog."

14. We can't wait to hear the song, which he wrote for jazz, his french poodle.

15. He's a very creative person, and he sings like sting.

16. The chorus 102 class will sing back-up with miss thompson.

17. we're calling the event springfield's fiesta fantastic.

18. The South end of the Gym is reserved for the Piñata bashing.

19. Springfield's fiesta Fantastic is scheduled for ~~jan~~ January 30.

20. the *Springfield daily* ~~*Trib*~~ Tribune. will come and take pictures.

21. what a great way to study the spanish-mexican cultures!

Next Step Remember or imagine a time when you and a teacher worked together on a project. It could have involved something fun like planning an assembly program or an end-of-the-year cleanup, or something as serious as organizing a tornado or fire drill. Write a paragraph or two about this experience. Exchange finished products with a partner and check carefully for capitalization and abbreviation errors.

Capitalization 1

For most people, capitalizing the first word in a sentence is pretty automatic. It is knowing when to capitalize all the other words that is the greater challenge. (Add to your capitalization know-how by becoming familiar with 404.1-407.3 in your *Write Source 2000* handbook, and then try the exercises that follow.)

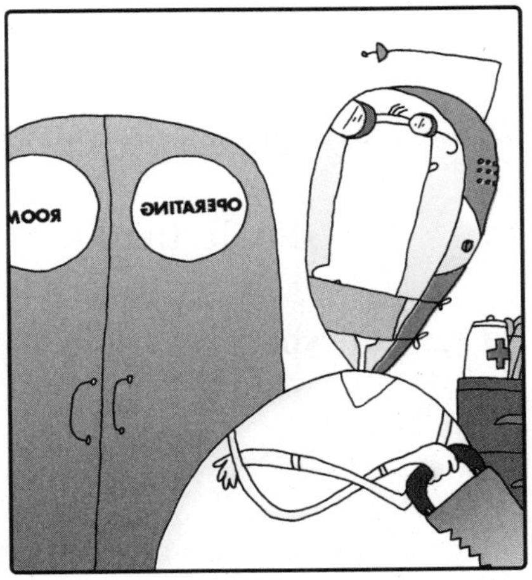

Directions **Underline the word or words that need capitalization in each sentence below. Then write each capitalized word or words in the space above the error. The first one has been done for you.**

Mayor William James
1. After the win, mayor william james arranged for a victory parade.

Uncle Bill
2. I went out and joined uncle bill, who was sitting on the porch steps.

Asian
3. Brody's interest in martial arts came from his study of asian culture.

American
4. My sister wrote a long paper for her american literature course.

Middle Ages
5. I would not want to have lived in the middle ages.

Dr. Karl Jacobs
6. The operation will be performed by dr. karl jacobs.

South
7. My brother found it hard to adjust to the slower pace of the south.

Flowers Algernon
8. I plan to read the short book *flowers for algernon* this weekend.

Spanish
9. Juan is helping me learn to speak and read spanish.

Easter
10. I don't know where our family is going for easter vacation.

African
11. My mother added to her collection of african art on her last trip to Kenya.

Green Bay Packers
12. How will the green bay packers do this year?

FBI
13. Eric didn't realize he was part of an fbi investigation.

All Write pp. 328-332

United Nations
14. When was the united nations formed?

Democratic Party
15. The democratic party was proud to have him as a member.

Interstate
16. You should take interstate 95 all the way into town.

Latin
17. Did you know you have to take a year of latin to graduate from some high schools?

Southern
18. My favorite part of the trip to Georgia was the southern cooking.

West Coast
19. How does the west coast compare to where you lived before?

Three Dog Night
20. I heard three dog night was recording a new album.

Pizza Hut Midway
21. After the game, everyone went to the pizza hut restaurant on midway

Boulevard
boulevard.

Big Mac
22. I would have preferred a big mac hamburger to pizza.

Washington Monument
23. Climbing to the top of the washington monument is one of my goals.

Directions

In the sentences below, put a line through any unnecessary capital letters and write the correct small letter above the line. The first sentence has been done for you.

e
1. The large truck turned ~~E~~ast at the edge of town.

m d h
2. My ~~M~~om and ~~D~~ad met Aunt Thelma at the ~~H~~ospital.

s
3. Next Tuesday will be the first day of ~~S~~pring.

m
4. Lucas hadn't counted on failing his ~~M~~ath test.

c
5. Wheatums ~~C~~ereal is my favorite breakfast food.

s s
6. To find the ~~S~~tadium, turn ~~S~~outh on North Avenue.

h s
7. The ~~H~~igh ~~S~~chool is located on Jackson Street.

Capitalization 2

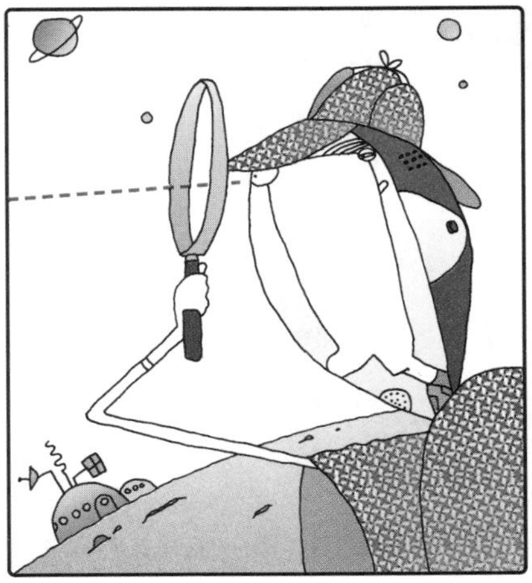

Here's another exercise to help you capitalize words correctly. (Turn to 404.1 - 407.3 in *Write Source 2000* for more information on capitalization.)

Directions **Each sentence below has at least one error in capitalization. There may be more than one error in some of the sentences. Underline each error and write the correction in the space above the line. The first sentence has been done for you.**

dad FBI New York City
1. Chen's Dad worked for the fbi in the new york city office.

World Trade Center
2. He investigated the world trade center bombing.

local police agencies New York City Police Department
3. The FBI often works with Local Police Agencies such as the new york city police department.

terrorism kidnapping
4. Crimes such as Terrorism and Kidnapping come under FBI jurisdiction.

The police departments
5. the FBI's advanced crime-fighting facilities are used by local Police Departments.

fingerprint file
6. The bureau keeps a Fingerprint File containing millions of fingerprints.

history law enforcement
7. Chen's dad talked to our History class when we studied Law Enforcement.

trial lawyer agent
8. He was a Trial Lawyer before becoming an FBI Agent.

J. Edgar Hoover's organized crime
9. He also told us stories about j. edgar hoover's fight against Organized Crime.

NASA IRS government organizations
10. Today the FBI works with nasa, the irs, and other Government Organizations.

Directions **For additional practice, find the errors in capitalization in the sentences below. There may be more than one error in each sentence. Underline each error and write the correction in the space above the line. (Refer to 404.4-407.3 in your *Write Source 2000* handbook for help.)**

professional
1. Someone once jokingly said that anyone who didn't like Professional
football *un*
Football was Un-American.

Super Bowl
2. Judging from the way people react each year to the super bowl, there are
loyal
millions of Loyal Americans.

Central High School *Football Hall of Fame*
3. Seniors from central high school are going to the football hall of fame in
Canton, Ohio *spring*
canton, ohio, during their senior trip this Spring.

Native American
4. My friend Danny is a native american, and he is very anxious to see what
the hall of fame contains about Jim Thorpe and other old-time players.

Danny *of*
5. danny just finished reading a book called *The Early Years Of the NFL*.

Billy *South*
6. My friend billy is from the south, and he wants to see all the quarterbacks
from southern colleges that are in the hall of fame.

Brett Favre
7. His current favorite player is brett favre, the quarterback who went to
Mississippi *Green Bay Packers*
college in mississippi and now plays for the green bay packers.

Next Step List three proper nouns for each of the following:

1. Names of people
2. Historical names
3. Abbreviations
4. Roads or highways
5. Titles used with names
6. Organizations
7. Public areas
8. Countries
9. Buildings

Capitalize the nouns. Share your list with a friend.

All Write pp. 328-332

Plurals and Spelling 1

Making the plural form of most nouns is easy. All you do is add *s* to the singular. But there are always exceptions. (Turn to 408.1 - 409.3 in your *Write Source 2000* handbook for more information.)

Directions

After each singular word below, write the plural form of the word. The first one has been done for you.

1. cup ___cups___
2. roof ___roofs___
3. mile ___miles___
4. sister-in-law ___sisters-in-law___
5. mouthful ___mouthfuls___
6. child ___children___
7. deer ___deer___
8. hoof ___hooves___
9. cry ___cries___
10. thief ___thieves___
11. loaf ___loaves___
12. solo ___solos___
13. box ___boxes___
14. pen ___pens___
15. pailful ___pailfuls___
16. monkey ___monkeys___
17. knife ___knives___
18. life ___lives___
19. key ___keys___
20. goose ___geese___
21. radio ___radios___
22. donkey ___donkeys___
23. fox ___foxes___
24. dress ___dresses___
25. piano ___pianos___
26. marker ___markers___
27. chief ___chiefs___
28. tomato ___tomatoes___
29. lunch ___lunches___
30. dish ___dishes___

All Write pp. 333-335

Plurals and Spelling 2

There are a number of rules for forming and spelling plurals correctly. There are also some general spelling rules to help you as you write. (Turn to 411.1 - 411.4 in your *Write Source 2000* handbook for this information.)

Directions **In the space next to each misspelled word below, write the correct spelling. Write *C* if the spelling is correct. The first one has been done for you.**

1. admitance	*admittance*	**9.** useful	*C*
2. prefered	*preferred*	**10.** acheive	*achieve*
3. ladys	*ladies*	**11.** trys	*tries*
4. happyness	*happiness*	**12.** trying	*C*
5. monkies	*monkeys*	**13.** niether	*neither*
6. weird	*C*	**14.** foriegn	*foreign*
7. neice	*niece*	**15.** huming	*humming*
8. useing	*using*	**16.** begining	*beginning*

Note: There are some exceptions to most of the spelling rules. Keep a list of these words, or try to memorize them. Also, review the hints for becoming a better speller in your *Write Source 2000* handbook.

Next Step Keep your own list of challenging words based on the spelling list in your handbook and your reading. Follow the steps to becoming a better speller until you master the first list. (Start with 10 words.) Have a classmate test your mastery of your words. Make a habit of adding and mastering new words each week. Be certain you know the meaning as well as the spelling for each word on your list.

Abbreviations and Numbers

Some abbreviations may be used in formal writing (*Ms., Mr., Mrs.*); others may not (*yr.* for *year*). (See examples below and also turn to 409.4-409.6 in your *Write Source 2000* handbook for additional information on abbreviations and when to use them. Then turn to 410.1-410.6 for basic rules covering the use of numbers.)

EXAMPLES

Abbreviation: **Mr.** (Mister)

Acronym: **CARE** (Cooperative for American Relief Everywhere)

Initialism: **CIA** (Central Intelligence Agency)

Decade: **1880s** (*not* eighteen eighties)

Specific Year: **1952** (*not* nineteen fifty-two)

Directions **Correct the errors in the use of abbreviations and numbers in the sentences below. Underline each error and write the correct form in the space above the error. The first sentence has been done for you.**

FBI *United States*
1. The f.b.i. has jurisdiction over federal crimes within the U.S.

1930's *dollars*
2. During the nineteen thirties, bank robbers stole thousands of $'s, and many of the robbers ended up on the bureau's "Most Wanted" list.

two
3. FBI agents caught 2 of the country's most famous bank robbers, John
and
Dillinger & Baby Face Nelson.

1924
4. After J. Edgar Hoover took charge in nineteen twenty-four, the FBI became more effective in fighting crime.

hundreds *year*
5. Mr. Hoover prosecuted 100's of criminals each yr.

All Write pp. 335 and 337

Six / two 5-page

6. 6 members of our school newspaper collaborated to write 2 5-pg. articles based on interviews with former FBI agents.

approximately / 60

7. They learned that approx. sixty agents out of every 100 had received training as either lawyers or accountants before joining the FBI.

Directions **Opposite each number below, list the matching common term or its abbreviation. Some of the answers may come from your general knowledge. (Some of the answers may be found on pages 247 and 409 in your *Write Source 2000* handbook.) The first one has been done for you.**

	Term	Abbreviation
1.	ante meridiem	*a.m. or A.M.*
2.	*highway*	HWY or hwy.
3.	*New York*	NY or N.Y.
4.	Doctor	*Dr.*
5.	compact disc	*CD*
6.	*World Wide Web*	WWW
7.	Boulevard	*Blvd. or BLVD*
8.	*Mister*	Mr.
9.	Alaska	*AK*
10.	post meridiem	*p.m. or P.M.*

Next Step Write five original sentences using numbers. Exchange your sentences with a classmate and edit each other's sentences for usage errors. If you find errors, discuss the corrections and review rules in your handbook.

All Write pp. 335-336

Mechanics Review

Directions **Read the paragraphs below carefully. Correct spelling and capital letters where necessary and also make corrections where needed in the use of plurals, abbreviations, and numbers. Underline any error and write the correction in the space above the error. The first sentence has been done for you. (See 404.1-411.4 in *Write Source 2000* as well as the instructions and examples at the top of page 49 in this *SkillsBook*.)**

last [Last] year my family moved from a small town in Northern [northern] ohio [Ohio] to New York city [City]. In the beginning, I was amazed at how different the states are—Ohio from New York—and how different the midwest [Midwest] is from the east [East], but I was really amazed at the difference between life in small-town america [America] and life in the big City [city]. A number of surprises came when I started attending High School [high school] in sept [September].

The 1st [first] surprise was the size of the school. The building seemed to take up an entire city block. The 2nd [second] surprise involved class sizes. 20 [Twenty] students was an average-sized class in William Howard Taft high [High], my old school; forty students was an average-sized class here at central high [Central High]. In addition to the sheer number of students, the number of different nationalities was incredible. I felt as if I had wandered into a meeting of the united nations [United Nations]. I met students from columbia [Columbia], India, and china [China] my first day in school, & [and] I discovered they were only a small % [percentage] of the more than fifty [50] different nationalities represented at this High School [high school]. While I was walking through the halls, I could hear a dozen different languages.

At lunch that first day, I met Harjot Singh, who came from India. I found out that Harjot lived in my nieghborhood [neighborhood]. he [He] was nice enough to invite me to his house to sample indian [Indian] cooking.

It was a good thing Harjot offered his help after schoool on that first day, too. If he hadn't, I might still be trying to figure out which Subway [subway] to take to get home. Astonished by how crowded it was at the station, I was frozen in confusion as carloads of passengers left the station. The map of subway routes provided by the transit authority was meaningless to me. It looked more like a diagram of the veins and arterys [arteries] in the human body than a map of train rts [routes].

Even when Harjot pointed out the right train, I almost missed it because I was listening to 3 [three] muscians playing banjoes [banjos]. A poke in the ribs from Harjot reminded me to pay more attention. A subway platform is no place to be daydreaming.

I found Harjot's advice and information about getting along in the city useful from the very begining [beginning]. Now that I have spent a full yr. [year] in new york [New York] at my new school, I have come to realize how helpful he was to me in 100 and one [101] different ways. I also am gratful [grateful] to Harjot's Mom [mom] for all that great indian [Indian] food.

Next Step Using your own paper, describe a time when you were in an unfamiliar situation and someone offered you assistance that really helped you out. Then, exchange papers with a friend and read his or her story carefully, underlining any errors. Once you get your story back, make any necessary corrections to your own work.

Using the Right Word 1

When is it important to know if one word (*good*) should be used instead of another word (*well*)? The answer to that is easy. It's important to use the right word whenever you are going to share your thoughts in a formal or semiformal situation. For example, whenever you write a report for a class, speak in front of any group, or write a letter requesting information, you should use the language correctly.

Test your word knowledge by trying the activity below. (If you find yourself in doubt about whether to replace a specific word, refer to sections 419.1-433.5 in your *Write Source 2000* handbook for more information.)

Directions **Draw a line through any incorrect underlined word and write the correct form above it. Do not change a word that is correct. The first sentence has been done for you.**

1. We formed a ~~counsel~~ *council* to decide on ~~witch~~ *which* items to put in a time capsule.
2. We knew we had limited space in the capsule we had made, so we ~~choose~~ *chose* many small items.
3. I ~~excepted~~ *accepted* many ideas from the other members of the class, and that ~~lead~~ *led* to some interesting discussions.
4. The teacher said that we had to be ~~vary~~ *very* sure that we didn't put in things that would ~~brake~~ *break*.
5. We needed to seal the items in plastic and force out all the ~~heir~~ *air*.
6. My dad told us the school ~~bored~~ *board* would like to ~~here~~ *hear* about this project.
7. I had to ~~by~~ *buy* some film to take photographs for the newspaper.

All Write pp. 345-360

8. We ~~through~~ *threw* in some bottle tops, some baseball cards, and some of my mom's ~~personnel~~ *personal* stationery.

9. As I held the capsule in my hand, I told everybody that the items ~~wood~~ *would* be worth ~~alot~~ *a lot* in the future.

10. The council decided that the year 2041 ~~wood~~ *would* be a good year ~~too~~ *to* open the capsule.

11. Instructions kept in the school safe will direct the ~~principle~~ *principal* to open the capsule in front of the whole school.

12. We painted the ~~steal~~ *steel* capsule bright ~~read~~ *red* and buried it between two walls.

13. The ~~counsel~~ *council* ~~maid~~ *made* a pact to visit the school on that "historic" day in 2041 and relive our ~~passed~~ *past*.

Next Step Write a sentence for each of the following pairs or sets of words: *accept, except; already, all ready; capital, capitol; fewer, less; principal, principle;* and *who, whom.* (Use one set of words per sentence.) Then check your word usage by looking up each word in your *Write Source 2000* handbook (sections 419.1-433.5). Make any necessary changes.

Using the Right Word 2

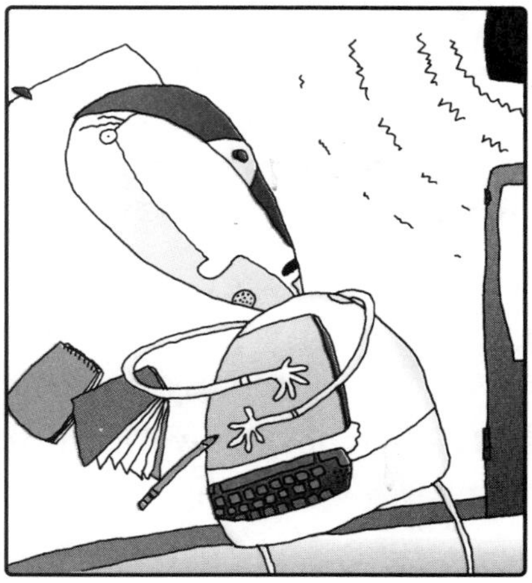

The next three activities will ask you to think carefully about specific words. You'll have to judge whether to use these words, or not use them, in particular sentences. (Sections 419.1-433.5 in your *Write Source 2000* handbook provide information about the words in these exercises as well as other commonly misused words.)

Directions **If the underlined word is incorrect, cross out the word and write the correct form above it.**

We had all ~~herd~~ heard the principal's voice ~~threw~~ through the public address system. ~~Their~~ There was no mistaking the announcement: "Students ~~that~~ who have lockers in the upper hall will have locker cleanup this morning."

"I knew I should have done that last ~~weak~~ week," I thought.

"~~Your~~ You're in for it now," snickered our homeroom teacher. Seeing our ~~paned~~ pained looks, teachers went ~~buy~~ by our lockers with encouraging words.

"Don't ~~let~~ leave those apples in ~~their~~ there any longer," ~~counciled~~ counseled one teacher.

Tami and Al, my ~~too~~ two neighbors, had already cleaned ~~there~~ their lockers.

"Give him some space there," said Mr. Gonzales. "He needs room."

"I don't ~~no~~ know how he could ~~leave~~ let that locker get so messy," Al said.

But the last laugh was on Mr. G., ~~four~~ for only ~~too~~ two minutes after we got back ~~too~~ to our homerooms, the vice-~~principle~~ principal announced that all eighth-grade students should check to see if ~~there~~ their teachers' desks were clean as well!

All Write pp. 345-360

Using the Right Word 3

Directions **Draw a line through any incorrect underlined word and write the correct form above it. Do not change a word that is correct. (Refer to sections 419.1-433.5 in your *Write Source 2000* handbook for information on using correct words.)**

1. We moved ~~two~~ *to* Elm Street, so our annual Halloween scavenger hunts are more fun ~~then~~ *than* ever.

2. Freddy—my friend—helped us ~~raze~~ *raise* money to ~~by~~ *buy* what we needed.

3. Although four teams of eighth-grade friends seemed like a large ~~amount~~ *number* of kids, we did manage to get them ~~altogether~~ *all together* on the evening of the hunt.

4. That evening when my mom ~~blue~~ *blew* the whistle, the games began.

5. Jim's team ~~lead~~ *led* early on by getting half of the items on the list from ~~Ant~~ *Aunt* Julia's house, including a ~~pare~~ *pair* of glass paperweights.

6. My best friend, Sam, did ~~good~~ *well* finding a stamp with a grizzly ~~bare~~ *bear* on it in a stack of ~~male~~ *mail* on the hall table.

7. Maya's team found an old ~~blew~~ *blue* tennis shoe in the ~~creak~~ *creek*.

8. It took my team ~~too~~ *two* hours before it finally found a Boy Scout troop ~~metal~~ *medal*.

9. But it was Sam ~~that~~ *who* won the contest by entering the ~~desserted~~ *deserted* house near the river and getting the Freddie Krueger glove I ~~through~~ *threw* in ~~their~~ *there* earlier.

10. We all complimented him on that ~~peace~~ *piece* of bravery.

Using the Right Word 4

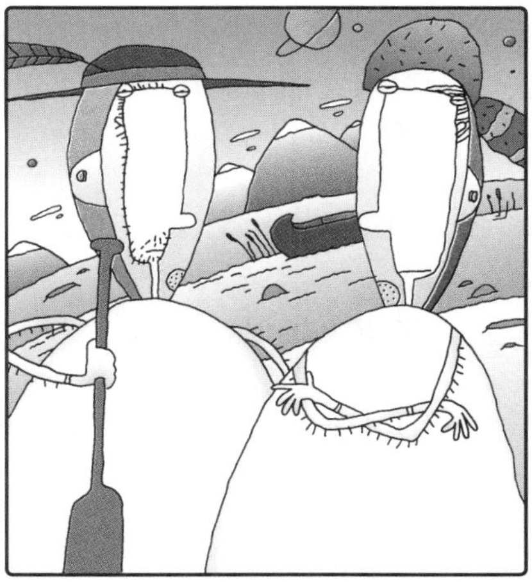

Many words that writers often find confusing are called **homophones.** Homophones are words that sound alike but are spelled differently. *To, two,* and *too* are homophones. (See 419.1-433.5 in your *Write Source 2000* handbook for information about commonly misused words. Some of those words will be homophones.)

Directions **Circle the correct word in each set of words. Among the sets there will be 16 pairs of homophones. Put *H* above each pair of homophones. The first sentence has been done for you.**

1. There have been many famous *(pears, pairs)* in history.
2. In 1804, Meriwether Lewis and William Clark *(lead, led)* an expedition *(who, that)* explored the western United States.
3. They *(choose, chose)* a route that followed the Missouri River, so they did not have to cross any *(deserts, desserts)*.
4. Lewis and Clark had traveled *(farther, further)* west *(than, then)* any other American explorers.
5. On the trip across the *(plain, plane)*, Sacajawea, a Shoshone woman, acted as *(a, an)* interpreter for the group.
6. After crossing *(through, threw)* the Oregon Territory, the explorers reached the Pacific Ocean, where they *(threw, through)* away *(there, their)* smelly, tattered clothes.

All Write pp. 345-360

7. The winter *(whether, weather)* wasn't very *(well, good)*, so the explorers rested.

8. The expedition split into *(two, to)* groups, and neither group went *(two, too)* far off *(coarse, course)*, returning to St. Louis in 1806.

9. Both groups returned to St. Louis with many tales to tell *(there, their)* families.

10. President Thomas Jefferson *(read, red)* their reports and gave each leader a *(metal, medal)*.

11. Today *(there, their)* is a museum in St. Louis dedicated to *(there, their)* trip.

12. The museum is at the *(base, bass)* of the Gateway Arch *(beside, besides)* the Mississippi River.

13. The land they explored is a *(vary, very)* important *(peace, piece)* of the United States.

Next Step Try writing a tongue twister using homophones that begin with the letter *b*. (See your handbook for help.)

Using the Right Word Review 1

Directions **Draw a line through any incorrect underlined word and write the correct form above it. Do not change a word that is correct. The first line has been done for you. (See 419.1-433.5 in your *Write Source 2000* handbook for information on using the right word.)**

When my dad was 15, he couldn't ~~weight~~ *wait* to have his dad ~~learn~~ *teach* him how ~~too~~ *to* drive. Last ~~weak~~ *week*, my grandfather ~~choose~~ *chose* to tell me the tale of my dad's first day behind the wheel.

"Jack, ~~its~~ *it's* a good day for your first lesson," said Grandpa John. After ~~alot~~ *a lot* of reminders about the "rules of the road," my grandpa and dad were ~~already~~ *all ready* to begin. On that fateful ~~mourning~~ *morning*, my grandfather said, "Son, let's get some practice in before the ~~whether~~ *weather* turns rainy." It must have been scary for Dad, ~~setting~~ *sitting* behind the wheel of Grandpa's new car.

With a chuckle Grandpa told me, "~~You're~~ *Your* dad's knees probably felt weak." He said that Dad needed ~~alot~~ *a lot* of reminding about ~~witch~~ *which* buttons and levers ~~too~~ *to* push and when to push them. Dad ~~seamed~~ *seemed* nervous ~~buy~~ *by* the time he was ready to pull out of the driveway, and he accidentally ~~blue~~ *blew* the horn. Grandpa admitted ~~their~~ *there* was some nervousness on his part, too. He tried to compliment Dad on everything he did ~~write~~ *right* as they safely ~~past~~ *passed* a slow-moving truck. Of ~~coarse~~ *course*, he ~~choose~~ *chose* to be positive with his son. But Grandpa admitted to me that every time my father came ~~too~~ *to* a stop, he hit his own imaginary ~~break~~ brake. Some miles farther down the road, Grandpa ~~herd~~ heard a gasp from the ~~knew~~ new driver. Dad ~~maid~~ made a turn ~~to~~ too soon and almost ran ~~rite~~ right into a parked car. Grandpa thought, "~~Its~~ It's not going to be a good day."

"After that, I kept picturing my new car as a mangled mass of ~~medal~~ metal," admitted my grandfather.

"Well, Grandpa, at least you weren't ~~board~~ bored with the driving lesson," I said.

Grandpa chuckled. "On the contrary," he said, "I almost fainted that day." Grandpa said that, if nothing else, he taught Dad a very important ~~principal~~ principle of driving: Keep ~~you're~~ your eyes on the road!

~~They're~~ There we were, both laughing, when Dad came out on the porch and sat ~~besides~~ beside me and asked what was up. Grandpa smiled at me and said, "Jack, before you ~~no~~ know it, you'll go ~~threw~~ through it yourself with little Johnny ~~hear~~ here." The next morning, Dad ~~razed~~ raised the question again about Grandpa's ~~personnel~~ personal comments.

"~~Its~~ It's almost time ~~four~~ for my first driving lesson," I replied casually. There was a sudden ~~paned~~ pained expression on Dad's face. He now realized it was his turn ~~two~~ to be the teacher and mine ~~too~~ to be the student.

Using the Right Word Review 2

Directions **In the following paragraphs, draw a line through any incorrectly used word and then write the correct usage above it. Read each sentence carefully before making any corrections. (See 419.1-433.5 in your *Write Source 2000* handbook for information on using the right word.)**

It has always ~~seamed too~~ seemed to me that cats make better pets ~~then~~ than dogs. ~~Its~~ It's not that I have anything ~~personnel~~ personal against dogs; ~~its~~ it's just that ~~their~~ they're more work ~~then~~ than cats. This is ~~vary~~ very true in the colder climates ~~wear~~ where walking a dog can be ~~vary~~ very uncomfortable. And, of ~~coarse~~ course, there's the ~~hole~~ whole issue of cleaning up after ~~you're~~ your dog. It can be a real ~~pane~~ pain!

Dogs are supposed to be smarter than cats. ~~Sum wood~~ Some would say that this is true because dogs can learn ~~alot~~ a lot of different tricks. I'm not ~~to~~ too sure I really ~~except~~ accept that argument. I think cats could learn as ~~good~~ well as dogs if they wanted ~~too~~ to. I think cats are just ~~to~~ too smart and independent to do what people want them to do on command.

For example, I once tried to ~~learn~~ teach my cat how to fetch when I ~~through~~ threw a ball. I kept trying, but it was a ~~waist~~ waste of time. Finally, I got tired and ~~quite~~ quit. As soon as I decided to drop the ball and ~~set~~ sit down, my cat grabbed the ball and dropped it in my lap. My cat was just showing me that he ~~wood~~ would do the trick when he ~~choose~~ chose to, not when I ordered him ~~too~~ to. ~~Sew~~ So what does that tell you about ~~witch~~ which animal is smarter?

Another thing that has always bothered me about dogs is the noise they make. In general cats are much more ~~quite then~~ [quiet than] dogs. Dogs will bark and howl at just about anything—if they ~~here~~ [hear] the stairs ~~creek~~ [creak] or a person delivering ~~male~~ [mail] or someone ~~pooring~~ [pouring] a glass of lemonade.

Dogs do serve ~~an amount~~ [a number] of useful purposes like helping the blind and tracking down lost children. But that's the point: ~~leave~~ [let] the dogs work; let the cats ~~lay~~ [lie] around shedding ~~there hare~~ [their hair] and just being good pets.

Sentence Activities

The activities in this section cover four important areas: (1) the basic parts, types, and kinds of sentences; (2) methods for writing smooth-reading sentences; (3) common sentence errors; and (4) ways to add variety to sentences. Most activities include a main practice part in which you review, combine, or analyze different sentences. In addition, the **Next Step** activities give you follow-up practice with certain skills.

Subjects and Predicates

A sentence consists of two parts: a subject and a predicate. The **subject** is the part of the sentence that is doing something or about which something is said. The **predicate** (or verb) is the part of the sentence that says something about the subject. Each sentence has a *simple subject* and a *complete subject* and a *simple predicate* and a *complete predicate.* (For more information, see 434.2-435.7 in *Write Source 2000.*)

EXAMPLE

The very idea of computers terrified my dad completely.

("Idea" is the simple subject of the sentence. "The very idea of computers" is the complete subject. "Terrified" is the simple predicate. "Terrified my dad completely" is the complete predicate.)

Directions

In each of the following sentences, place parentheses around the simple subject and draw a line under the complete subject. Draw a circle around the simple predicate and draw a double line under the complete predicate. (*Note:* A simple subject or predicate may also serve as the complete subject or predicate.) The first sentence has been done for you.

1. My younger (sister) convinced Dad to get a computer.
2. (Dad) stared at the box the computer arrived in without touching it.
3. (He) looked at the box as if expecting it to explode.
4. (I) assembled the components under Dad's suspicious gaze.
5. Our brand-new (monitor) blinked to life.
6. My dad's (mistrust) of the computer lessened over the next few weeks.
7. His computer-generated (report) looked great with colorful graphics.

All Write pp. 368-369

Directions **In each of the following sentences, place parentheses around the simple subject and draw a line under the complete subject. Draw a circle around the simple predicate and draw a double line under the complete predicate. The first sentence has been done for you.**

1. Violent (thunderstorms) hit my hometown during the summer.
2. The first few (storms) had been typical summer rains.
3. The (storms) became more intense by late June.
4. Storm (warnings) were given almost daily throughout the month of July.
5. (It) was hard to plan ahead.
6. An uneasy (feeling) was settling in throughout the town.
7. The (feeling) grew stronger every day.
8. (People) began acting in unusual ways.
9. (Bob) jumped nervously at every sudden sound.
10. Showing how upset he was, (Dan) snapped at his little brother.
11. (Mary) heard strange noises around her house after dark.
12. (Everyone) was hearing strange things.
13. (Things) started to return to normal by early August.
14. (It) was a summer to remember.

Next Step Write three sentences describing either a rainstorm or a snowstorm. Then in each sentence (1) put parentheses around your simple subject, (2) draw a line under the complete subject, (3) draw a circle around your simple predicate, and (4) draw a double line under the complete predicate. Now read your simple sentences without any of the modifiers. Have you met the sentence requirement? Is there a subject (noun or pronoun) and predicate (verb) in each sentence?

Compound Subjects and Predicates

A sentence that contains two or more simple subjects has a **compound subject.** A sentence that contains two or more simple predicates has a **compound predicate.** A sentence may have a compound subject, a compound predicate, or both. (Turn to 434.2 - 435.7 and 437.4 in *Write Source 2000* for more information.)

Note: Do not confuse a simple sentence containing compound subjects or compound predicates with a compound sentence. A compound sentence contains *two simple sentences* joined by a comma with a coordinating conjunction or joined by a semi-colon. A compound sentence has a subject and a verb in each independent clause.

EXAMPLES

Compound Subject:
Carlos and Andre love pasta.

Compound Predicate:
Carlos eats fettuccini and devours tortellini.

Compound Sentence:
I like pasta, but meatballs make me ill.

Directions **In the following sentences, underline the simple or compound subjects with one line and the simple or compound predicates with two lines. In the blank before each sentence, label a simple sentence *S* and a compound sentence *C*. The first sentence has been done for you.**

C 1. Sheri and Aretha spoke at the meeting, and Mary took notes.

S 2. I fell asleep and missed the meeting.

S 3. You can watch television or finish your homework.

S 4. Bill and Jim bought a new board and played darts for hours.

S 5. Billy played hard but lost the game anyway.

 All Write pp. 368-369 and 372

C 6. The ship sank, but the crew launched the lifeboats and escaped.

S 7. Carlos, Juan, and Nancy were finalists in the poster contest.

C 8. I liked Juan's poster, but the judges awarded the prize to Carlos.

S 9. Bacon and eggs is a standard American breakfast.

S 10. The green and white car skidded and swerved down the street.

S 11. John, Bill, and Juan joined the Fox River Chess Club and played every Thursday afternoon.

C 12. The Dale twins looked alike, and they often dressed alike, too.

S 13. The boy with red hair delivered newspapers up and down the street.

S 14. Would you please open the window and air the smoke out of this room?

C 15. The lake shimmers a thousand gleaming lights by day, but it is dark and still at night.

S 16. The weary group of hikers trudged up the hill and down the valley.

Next Step Write five sentences describing a hike or trip you took. Make sure each sentence has a compound subject or compound verb (or both). Then in each sentence, underline the simple or compound subjects with one line and the simple or compound predicates with two lines.

Phrases and Clauses 1

Phrases and clauses are like a series of building blocks in the process of making sentences. **Phrases** are related groups of words lacking a subject or predicate (or both). Phrases can serve the same purposes as single words. Then there are clauses. **Clauses** are related groups of words that have a subject and a predicate. (Turn to 436.3 - 437.2 in *Write Source 2000* for more information.)

EXAMPLES

Phrases:

the startling new book = noun phrase (It has no predicate.)

had been written = verb phrase (It has no subject.)

in six months = prepositional phrase (It has no subject or predicate.)

Independent Clause:

The startling new book had been written in six months.

An *independent clause* has a subject and a predicate. It can stand as a sentence because it contains a complete thought and makes sense.

Dependent Clause:

Since the startling new book had been written in six months . . .

A *dependent clause* has a subject and predicate, but it cannot stand as a sentence because it depends on another part of the sentence to form a complete thought.

Directions **Label each group of words below as a phrase or clause. Write *P* in front of the group of words if it is a phrase; write *IC* for an independent clause or write *DC* for a dependent clause. The first one has been done for you.**

P **1.** ran down the hill

P **2.** the man with the big smile

DC **3.** when he saw the results of the race

DC **4.** after the rain had stopped

P **5.** having been thoroughly soaked

IC **6.** I finally bought a raincoat

DC **7.** which was supposed to be guaranteed weatherproof

P **8.** standing on the corner

P **9.** waiting for the bus

P **10.** patiently with 50 other people

Directions **Choose five of the phrases or dependent clauses from the exercise above. Then use them to create five independent clauses that can stand as individual sentences in the spaces provided below. (*Note:* You can combine the exercise material or add your own words to make your sentences.)**

1. *Answers will vary.* ____________________

____

2. ____________________

____

3. ____________________

____

4. ____________________

____

5. ____________________

____

Next Step Try writing the wackiest sentence you can based on the material in the exercise. (Combine the exercise material, if you like, or add your own words to make your sentence.) See who can write the funniest sentence in your class.

Phrases and Clauses 2

Sentences are composed of phrases and clauses. A phrase is a group of related words that lacks either a subject or a predicate (or both). (Turn to 436.3 - 437.2 in *Write Source 2000* to review phrases and clauses.)

EXAMPLES

Phrases:

crossed the street
(The phrase does not have a subject.)

the small boy in the green coat
(The phrase does not have a predicate.)

about five feet away
(The phrase does not have a subject or a predicate.)

Independent Clause:

The small boy in the green coat crossed the street.

An *independent clause* has a subject and a predicate. It can stand as a sentence because it contains a complete thought and makes sense.

Dependent Clause:

When the small boy in the green coat crossed the street . . .

A *dependent clause* has a subject and predicate, but it cannot stand as a sentence because it depends on another part of the sentence to form a complete thought.

Directions **In the blank in front of each group of words below, label each phrase with a *P*. Label each independent clause with *IC* and each dependent clause with *DC*. The first one has been done for you.**

DC **1.** When my grandma went to elementary school

P **2.** Country school with only two rooms for grades 1 through 6

P **3.** Thirty students in the entire school

IC **4.** Grades 1 through 3 were in one room

P **5.** Grades 4 through 6 in the other

IC **6.** The schoolrooms were heated by wood-burning stoves

IC **7.** Two teachers arrived early each morning to start the stoves

DC **8.** Before students arrived

IC **9.** Classes started at 8:00 a.m. and ended at 4:00 p.m.

P **10.** Fifteen-minute recess in the middle of the morning

P **11.** Played games in the school yard

DC **12.** Because swings and seesaws are popular among younger students

IC **13.** Some older students helped teachers

P **14.** Younger students with their lessons

IC **15.** Coming in from recess, they were cold

DC **16.** After they warmed their hands by the stove

IC **17.** They had to write spelling words on a slate

P **18.** Tried not to waste paper

IC **19.** Math was done on the slate, too

P **20.** Grandma home for lunch

IC **21.** Older students learned to use a quill pen

IC **22.** School was hard but a lot of fun, according to Grandma

Next Step How would you like to attend a two-room country schoolhouse like the one outlined in the exercise above? Write a paragraph describing why you would or wouldn't want to attend such a school. You might also want to talk to your grandparents, or some other people who are older, to find out what it was like when they went to school.

Misplaced Modifiers

Making certain your sentences are clear is a critical part of writing well. **Misplaced modifiers** occur when a modifying word or phrase is placed too far away from the word it modifies in the sentence. When that happens, either the modifier seems to modify a word that it cannot sensibly modify, or it is left without any word to modify at all. (For more information, turn to page 91 in *Write Source 2000*.)

EXAMPLE

Misplaced Modifier:

People driving a car with long hair should keep their windows closed.

(The sentence incorrectly states that the car has long hair.)

Corrected Version:

People with long hair should keep their windows closed while driving a car.

(It is now clear that it is people who have long hair.)

Directions **Rewrite each of the sentences below. Correct the errors in modifiers by moving the modifier closer to the word it should modify or by adding or changing words in the sentence. The first sentence has been done for you.** *Answers will vary.*

1. The girl in the car with long blond hair waved at Alex.

   The girl with long blond hair waved at Alex from the car.

2. Screaming and shrieking, I discovered the boy running down the highway.

   I discovered the boy running down the highway screaming and shrieking.

3. To make the team, coaches recommend that you practice long and hard.

   Coaches recommend that you practice long and hard to make the team.

4. I chased Dan as he jogged around the track on my scooter.

I chased Dan on my scooter as he jogged around the track.

5. I could see Mrs. Smith trimming her flowers from the open doorway.

From the open doorway, I could see Mrs. Smith trimming her flowers.

6. Hanging on for dear life, the bicycle crashed into the shrubbery.

As I was hanging on for dear life, the bicycle crashed into the shrubbery.

7. Wandering down the hall, the baked chicken smelled wonderful.

As I wandered down the hall, the baked chicken smelled wonderful.

8. To achieve good grades, teachers will tell you to listen carefully.

Teachers will tell you to listen carefully if you want to achieve good grades.

9. Buried under a pile of clothes, I found my old sweater.

I found my old sweater buried under a pile of clothes.

Next Step Explain why a favorite fictional character from a book, a film, or a TV program appeals to you. Underline each modifying phrase you use and draw an arrow from the phrase to the word it modifies. Avoid any misplaced or dangling modifiers.

Types of Sentences 1

There are four basic types of sentences: **simple, compound, complex,** and **compound-complex.** Each type is determined by the number of clauses—as well as the kind of clauses—used in it. Remember, clauses can be either independent or dependent. An independent clause can stand alone as a sentence. A dependent clause cannot. (Turn to 436.3 in *Write Source 2000* for more information on clauses and 437.3-438.2 for information on sentence types.)

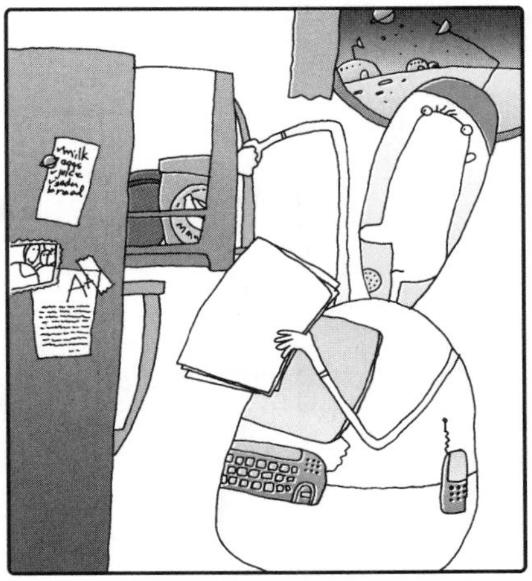

EXAMPLES

Simple Sentence:

John's story gave me goosebumps.

(one independent clause)

Compound Sentence:

John has a great imagination, and I always enjoy his writing.

(two or more independent clauses joined by a comma and a coordinate conjunction or joined by a semicolon)

Complex Sentence:

After John writes a story, he lets it "cool" for a few days.

(one independent clause and one or more dependent clauses)

Compound-Complex Sentence:

Although I don't write nearly as well as John, my writing is getting better, and extra work will improve it even more.

(two or more independent clauses and one or more dependent clauses)

Note: A simple sentence can have a compound subject or a compound verb. Do not confuse it with a compound sentence—a sentence that has two independent clauses.

Directions **Read each sentence below carefully. Label each sentence type on the line (*simple, compound, complex,* or *compound-complex*). The first one has been done for you.**

___simple___ **1.** Dawn and Rose watched the concert on TV last night.

___compound___ **2.** It featured a reunion of Three Dog Night, and the singers looked really old.

compound ________ **3.** I wonder what today's singers will look like in 20 years; most of them will be older than my dad is now.

complex ________ **4.** It would be weird to see male singers with only as much hair as my dad has.

compound-complex ________ **5.** My dad has a beard, and he always claims that the hair missing on his head just decided to grow on his face instead.

complex ________ **6.** Because he has had the beard for so long, I can't remember what he looked like without it.

simple ________ **7.** My dad with hair and young male singers without hair are equally hard to imagine.

complex ________ **8.** After I saw that concert, I decided not to watch any more TV reunion concerts for a while.

Directions **In the space provided below, write an example of each type of sentence. Try using your simple sentence as a base for the other, more complicated sentences.**

1. (*simple*) ________

2. (*compound*) ________

____

3. (*complex*) ________

____

4. (*compound-complex*) ________

____

____

Types of Sentences 2

Sentences are categorized by how they are put together (*form*), and the form is determined by the type and number of clauses a sentence contains. How the clauses—dependent or independent—are combined determines the type of sentence. (The four types of sentences are shown in the examples below and are also discussed in 437.3-438.2 in your *Write Source 2000* handbook.)

EXAMPLES

Simple Sentence:
I passed the English test with an "A."
(one independent clause)

Compound Sentence:
I passed the English test with an "A," and my parents were very happy.
I passed the English test with an "A"; my parents were very happy.
(two or more independent clauses joined by a comma and a coordinate conjunction or joined by a semicolon)

Complex Sentence:
When my parents are happy, I am happy.
(one independent clause and one or more dependent clauses)

Compound-Complex Sentence:
If I want to keep my parents happy, I should keep passing my English tests, and it might be a good idea to pass my math tests, too.
(two or more independent clauses and one or more dependent clauses)

Directions **For each sentence that follows, label its sentence type in the space provided (*simple, compound, complex, compound-complex*). The first sentence has been done for you.**

complex **1.** My friend Bob is a fanatic when it comes to collecting comics.

simple **2.** Bob puts each comic in a plastic cover and files all the comics in special boxes.

All Write p. 372

compound **3.** He has been collecting comics for about three years now, and his collection takes up almost all the available space in his attic.

complex **4.** He explained to me that the comics are very fragile and can easily be damaged if they aren't protected or if they are handled too much.

simple **5.** The scarcity of a comic and its condition determine its value.

simple **6.** The big event for Bob every year is the comic-book convention, Com-Con, in Chicago.

simple **7.** His big thrill at the convention this year was talking to artists Frank Miller and Todd McFarlane and getting them to autograph copies of his comic books.

complex **8.** Even though Bob has been offered quite a bit of money for some of his comics, he has never parted with a single one.

compound-complex **9.** Despite having to be so careful, Bob still loves reading his comics, and he also loves the whole process of searching for new additions to his collection, which is the thing I find hard to understand.

Next Step Clip a comic figure out of a newspaper and write a paragraph describing that character. Try to use a variety of sentence forms—*simple, compound, complex, compound-complex*—in your paragraph. When you have finished, read your paragraph to a friend and ask him or her to draw the character based on what they have read. If your friend draws a rough picture of your character and then can identify who it is, you are a success. If not, go back and add some details to your paragraph.

Kinds of Sentences 1

Sentences can be defined by the number and types of clauses they contain (*form*). Another way of defining sentences is by what they do (*function*). Each kind of sentence has a specific job to do and, based on that job, will use a specific kind of end punctuation. (For more information, see 438.3-438.6 in your *Write Source 2000* handbook.)

EXAMPLES

Declarative Sentence:

I write my e-mail on WebTV.

(A declarative sentence makes a statement about a person, a place, a thing, or an idea and ends with a period.)

Imperative Sentence:

Use the "power off" command to shut off the TV.

(An imperative sentence gives a command and often has an understood subject: *you.*)

Exclamatory Sentence:

I got 20 e-mail messages in one day!

(An exclamatory sentence expresses strong emotion or surprise and ends with an exclamation point.)

Interrogative Sentence:

Did Uncle Steve answer your e-mail?

(An interrogative sentence asks a question and ends with a question mark.)

Directions **Identify the sentences in the paragraph that follows. Decide the purpose of each sentence in the paragraph. Place a capital letter at the beginning of each sentence and then insert the correct punctuation mark at the end of the sentence. The first sentence has been done for you.**

last week we had a substitute English teacher for three days her name was Ms. Helms wow, was she nervous on her first day how did I know she was nervous all I had to do was look at her hand when she wrote on the blackboard her hand was shaking so badly she almost dropped the chalk. her voice squeaked when she tried to talk, and she kept looking at the door as though she expected someone to arrive to rescue her. the entire class could feel her nervousness. everyone in the class tried to act normally to avoid upsetting her any more. apparently what we considered normal wasn't much help. when Billy accidentally dropped a book on the floor, Ms. Helms jumped about a foot straight up in the air. after she had gone, we discovered Ms. Helms had never been in front of a class before. the class was actually happy to hear the familiar tones of our regular teacher when she returned after three days. at least we didn't have to worry about causing her to have a nervous breakdown. (or) !

Directions **Pretend that you are a substitute teacher in front of a class for the first time. Write about your experience using the four kinds of sentences below. You may put the sentences in any order, but be sure to use correct end punctuation. (Check each sentence off after you use it.)**

☐ **Declarative** ☐ **Imperative** ☐ **Exclamatory** ☐ **Interrogative**

Kinds of Sentences 2

Sentences are classified by what they do (*function*). Some sentences make a statement **(declarative);** some ask a question **(interrogative);** some give a command **(imperative);** and some express strong emotion **(exclamatory).** Also, some sentences, especially imperative sentences, have understood subjects. (Turn to 438.3-438.6 in *Write Source 2000* for more information.)

EXAMPLE

Please close the door. or **Please close the door!**
"You" is the understood subject of these sentences.

Directions

Place the proper punctuation at the end of each sentence below. Be sure to determine the function of the sentence based on the meaning and tone of the words. (*Note:* Some declarative and imperative sentences can become exclamatory sentences by using an exclamation point instead of a period.)

"Please close the door quickly!"

"Should I lock it?"

"Yes, and quickly!"

"How do I lock it?"

"Here, let me show you."

"Wow, don't close the door on my hand! I need that hand to use the periscope."

"Would I ever close the door on your hand?"

"No, you would never dream of such a thing, would you?"

"Not usually, but wouldn't you be surprised if I did?"

"I don't think I'd be surprised at anything you did!"

Directions In the space below, write a dialogue that might take place between two characters. The dialogue can be similar to the one in the previous exercise. Place proper punctuation—punctuation that fits the purpose of the sentence—at the end of each sentence.

Sentence Combining with Key Words

Ideas from two or three shorter sentences can be combined by moving a key word from one sentence to the other. A key word may be an adjective, an adverb, a compound adjective, or a participle. (Turn to page 94 in *Write Source 2000* for more information.)

EXAMPLE

The pizza was just baked. + The cheese was bubbling. + The cheese was hot.

The cheese on the just-baked pizza was bubbling hot.

(In this example, three short sentences have been combined into one. Key words *just* and *baked* become a compound adjective. The key word *bubbling* is a participle.)

Directions **In each pair of sentences, underline the key word(s) in the second sentence and then move it to the first. The first one has been done for you.**

1. Pizza dough can be tossed into the air. It should be tossed gently.

   Pizza dough can be tossed gently into the air.

2. Good pizzas are covered with cheese. The cheese should be gooey.

   Good pizzas are covered with gooey cheese.

3. Peppers add color and taste to a cheese pizza. Red ones are colorful.

   Red peppers add color and taste to a cheese pizza.

4. Mozzarella cheese is made from skim milk. The milk has no fat.

   Mozzarella cheese is made from no-fat skim milk.

5. Those homemade pizzas were delicious. They were topped with pepperoni.

   Those homemade pepperoni pizzas were delicious.

6. Pesto sauce looks strange on pizza. Pesto sauce is green.

   Green pesto sauce looks strange on pizza.

All Write p. 56

7. Sometimes pizza tastes good for breakfast. The pizza should be cold.

Sometimes cold pizza tastes good for breakfast.

8. Many restaurants have Italian-sounding names. These restaurants serve pizza.

Many pizza restaurants have Italian-sounding names.

9. The chef baked a pizza. He was scowling.

The scowling chef baked a pizza.

10. The pizza was too hot to eat. It was steaming.

The steaming pizza was too hot to eat.

11. Pizza delivery people drive fast. They drive extremely fast.

Pizza delivery people drive extremely fast.

12. My brother got a job as a restaurant mascot. He got it Friday.

Friday, my brother got a job as a restaurant mascot.

13. It is hot and smelly inside the mascot's costume. The costume is insulated.

It is hot and smelly inside the mascot's insulated costume.

14. The mascot waved to the children. The mascot was smiling.

The smiling mascot waved to the children.

Next Step Write five short sentences using the following subjects: (1) The girl . . . (2) The boy . . . (3) The teacher . . . (4) The dog . . . (5) The monster . . . . Pair up your sentences with a classmate's. Then use key words to combine the sentence pairs. Don't worry if some of the new sentences don't seem very logical. The idea is to combine the sentences with key words.

Sentence Combining with Phrases

Readers expect a certain amount of substance and rhythm in a piece of writing. Their expectations aren't met if the writing is full of choppy sentences. That's why sentence-combining exercises can be so helpful. They give you practice producing sentences with enough body and form to keep readers interested in your ideas. See the examples below. (Also, turn to page 95 in *Write Source 2000* for additional explanations and examples.)

EXAMPLES

Infinitive Phrase:
I ran to see the first pitch.
(*To see* is an infinitive phrase.)

Prepositional Phrase:
I ran to the bleachers.
(*To the bleachers* is a prepositional phrase.)

Appositive Phrase:
I ran to the bleachers, my usual spot.
(*My usual spot* is an appositive phrase renaming "bleachers.")

Participial Phrase:
Worried about being late, I ran to the bleachers.
(*Worried about being late* is a participial phrase describing "I.")

Combined Sentence:

Worried about being late, I ran to the bleachers, my usual spot, to see the first pitch.

Directions **Combine each pair of short sentences using the type of phrase indicated in parentheses. (Share your results.)**

1. I returned the stale Gummi Bears candy. It had been purchased at Ralph's Candy Shack. **(participial phrase)**

I returned the stale Gummi Bears candy purchased at Ralph's Candy Shack.

2. We rode in the stretch limousine. It was the one with the gold-plated wheel covers. **(prepositional phrase)**

We rode in the stretch limousine with the gold-plated wheel covers.

3. Jerome's idea doesn't surprise me at all. His idea is to run full speed into the ice-cold water. **(infinitive phrase)**

Jerome's idea to run full speed into the ice-cold water doesn't surprise me at all.

4. My neighbor took me for a short flight in his private plane. He is a commercial pilot. **(appositive phrase)**

My neighbor, a commercial pilot, took me for a short flight in his private plane.

5. My older brother already left. He left for his first steel guitar lesson. **(prepositional phrase)**

My older brother already left for his first steel guitar lesson.

6. The plot was discovered and stopped. The plot was to "toilet paper" my friend's house. **(infinitive phrase)**

The plot to "toilet paper" my friend's house was discovered and stopped.

7. The chapter is the one on photosynthesis. It is the one to read carefully. **(infinitive phrase)**

The chapter to read carefully is the one on photosynthesis.

Next Step Spend 3 to 5 minutes writing about what you eat when you are really, really hungry. (You may exaggerate a little.) As you review your writing, combine ideas as necessary to help your sentences read more effectively. Then exchange "menus" with a classmate.

Sentence Combining with a Series of Words or Phrases

Similar ideas from several short sentences can be combined into one sentence using a series of words or phrases. The words or phrases in a series should be stated in the same way (should be parallel) so that the sentence does not sound awkward. (Turn to page 94 in *Write Source 2000* for more information.)

EXAMPLE

The soccer fans were loud. They were rowdy. They destroyed things.
The soccer fans were *loud, rowdy,* and *destructive.*
(The words in the series are parallel. *Loud, rowdy,* and *destructive* are all adjectives.)

Directions **Check off the words or phrases in each sentence below that will make each series parallel. The first one has been done for you. *Important Note:* The last item in the series is always correct.**

1. At the start of the World Series, the crowd sang the national anthem

   __✔__ loudly, __✔__ proudly, _____ bad, and off-key.

2. The umpire yelled "Play ball" in a

   _____ not pleasant sounding, __✔__ loud, __✔__ raspy, and monotone voice.

3. The veteran pitcher was

   __✔__ winding up, __✔__ watching the catcher, _____ sneaky, and checking first base.

4. He fired a split-finger fastball that

   __✔__ curved in, _____ is doing funny things, __✔__ dropped off, and tailed away.

5. The batter hit the ball to the shortstop who

   __✔__ charged, __✔__ scooped, __✔__ jumped, and threw in time for the out.

Directions **Combine the ideas in the shorter sentences into one sentence that contains a series of parallel words or phrases. The first one has been done for you.**

1. "That pitch was inside," argued the manager. "And it was high and tight."

   "That pitch was inside, high, and tight," argued the manager.

2. The announcer yelled, "That ball is going. It's still going. It's gone!"

   The announcer yelled, "That ball is going, going, gone!"

3. The batter hit a home run. He hit a single and a triple, too.

   The batter hit a home run, a single, and a triple.

4. The team's uniform has a red jersey. The cap is blue, and the pants are white and gray.

   The team's uniform has a red jersey, a blue cap, and white and gray pants.

5. The old stadium has a crumbling wall. Its roof leaks, and its seats wobble.

   The old stadium has a crumbling wall, a leaky roof, and wobbly seats.

6. The umpire called, "There's one ball. There's one strike. There's one out."

   The umpire called, "There's one ball, one strike, and one out."

7. The relief pitcher scowled and stared. He kicked and threw.

   The relief pitcher scowled, stared, kicked, and threw.

8. That pitcher throws a blazing fastball. He has a sharp curveball. He also throws a sinking slider.

   That pitcher throws a blazing fastball, a sharp curveball, and a sinking slider.

Next Step Think of a sports figure that you admire. Write a list of words that describe him or her. Combine three or more similar words in a parallel series and use the series in a sentence.

Combining with Longer Sentences

Words like *after, although, before,* and *unless* carry a lot of meaning. They tell you when, how, and under what conditions the main action of a sentence happens. These words are **subordinate conjunctions,** and they are used to form complex sentences.

The group of words introduced by the subordinate conjunction is called an **adverb clause,** and it can come at the beginning or at the end of a sentence. This all sounds more complex than it is. The best way to understand adverb clauses is to see some examples. (Turn to page 96 in *Write Source 2000* and see the examples below.)

EXAMPLES

Chris made sure he had enough money. He bought a CD.
(Here are two short sentences.)

Before he bought a CD, **Chris made sure he had enough money.**
(The adverb clause is at the beginning of the sentence—a comma is needed.)

Chris made sure he had enough money *before he bought a CD*.
(The adverb clause is at the end of the sentence—no comma is needed.)

Directions **Combine the following short sentences into one sentence using the subordinate conjunction given in parentheses. The first one has been done for you.**

1. I was only four years old. I started kindergarten. **(when)**

   I was only four years old when I started kindergarten. Or . . . When I was only four years old, I started kindergarten.

2. She checked her numbers. The woman realized she held a winning lottery ticket. **(as)**

   As she checked her numbers, the woman realized she held a winning lottery ticket.

3. I tried to stay calm. My heart was pounding. **(although)**

Although my heart was pounding, I tried to stay calm.

(Or) I tried to stay calm although my heart was pounding.

4. Kyna smiled innocently. She hadn't done anything wrong. **(as though)**

Kyna smiled innocently as though she hadn't done anything wrong.

5. Bernadette felt lousy. She had lost her favorite necklace. **(because)**

Bernadette felt lousy because she had lost her favorite necklace.

6. Mark said he'd go to the party. He had to ask his parents' permission. **(use your own subordinate conjunction)**

After Mark said he'd go to the party, he had to ask his parents' permission.

7. I winced. I saw the math exam. **(use your own)**

I winced when I saw the math exam.

8. Mom left a note on the door. Dad would know where we went. **(use your own)**

Mom left a note on the door so that Dad would know where we went.

Next Step Write a paragraph or two about what happened this morning between the time you got up and the time you got to school. Try to put in as much detail as you can. Then exchange your writing with a classmate. Note ideas in one another's work that could be combined using adverb clauses.

Sentence Combining with Adjective Clauses

Too many "who's," "which's," and "that's" in your writing can make it sound wordy and impersonal. However, **relative pronouns** used in moderation can help you combine your ideas into more effective sentences. (The part of a complex sentence beginning with *who, which,* or *that* is called an **adjective clause.**) (Turn to page 96, and sections 444.1 and 433.1 in *Write Source 2000* for more information.)

EXAMPLES

Simple Sentences:
The bookstore barely held all the people. The people came to see Hank Aaron.
(*People* is unnecessarily repeated in these sentences.)

Combined Sentence:
The bookstore barely held all the people who came to see Hank Aaron.
(The repetition of *people* is avoided.)

Simple Sentences:
Aaron signed his book called *I Had a Hammer.* The book had just been released.
(*Book* is unnecessarily repeated.)

Combined Sentence:
Aaron signed his book called *I Had a Hammer,* which had just been released.
(The repetition of *book* is avoided.)

Directions **Study the two combined sentences above and determine why a comma is used in the second sentence and not in the first one. State your reason on the following lines. (Share your reason with a classmate. Then read the explanation of nonrestrictive phrases and clauses at 392.2 in your *Write Source 2000* handbook.)**

____

____

____

____

Directions **Combine each pair of sentences below into one complex sentence using *who, which,* or *that* as connectors. *Note:* Key words and punctuation marks have already been put in place.**

1. My dad talked about buying Hank Aaron's new autobiography. My dad enjoys reading about sports figures.

   My dad, who *enjoys reading about sports figures*,

   talked *about buying Hank Aaron's new autobiography*.

2. There was already a line when we arrived at the bookstore. That line went all the way around the block.

   There *was already a line* that *went all the way around the*

   block when we arrived at the bookstore.

3. We were in line for almost two hours. Two hours is a long time when you're hungry and there's no hot-dog stand in sight!

   We *were in line for almost two hours*,

   which *is a long time when you're hungry and there's no*

   hot-dog stand in sight!

4. Hank Aaron signed books continually. Hank Aaron stayed an hour longer than scheduled.

   Hank Aaron, who *stayed an hour longer than scheduled*,

   signed books continually.

5. My dad was very disappointed. My dad never did get Hank Aaron's autograph.

   My dad, who *never did get Hank Aaron's autograph*,

   was very disappointed.

Next Step Conduct an informal study. Circle or list all of the "who's," "which's," and "that's" you can find on one page of a textbook, magazine, or newspaper. Did you find many? How did it affect the level or feel of the language?

Sentence Combining with Compound Subjects and Verbs

By using compound subjects and compound verbs, you can combine ideas from shorter sentences into one sentence. A compound subject includes two or more subjects, and a compound verb includes two or more verbs. (Turn to page 95 in *Write Source 2000* for more information.)

EXAMPLES

Two Shorter Sentences:
A moose ran through our campsite. A squirrel ran through our campsite.

Combined Sentence with Compound Subject:
A moose and a squirrel ran through our campsite.

Two Shorter Sentences:
The squirrel opened an acorn. It ate the acorn.

Combined Sentence with Compound Verb:
The squirrel opened and ate an acorn.

Directions **Combine the following shorter sentences in each example into one sentence having a compound subject or a compound verb.**

1. Baby moose are called calves. Baby elk and cattle are called calves.

   Baby moose, elk, and cattle are called calves.

2. A full-grown moose stands six feet tall. It weighs around 1,000 pounds.

   A full-grown moose stands six feet tall and weighs around 1,000 pounds.

3. A bull moose's antlers grow all summer. They can weigh 75 pounds.

   A bull moose's antlers grow all summer and can weigh 75 pounds.

4. Moose eat tree bark and twigs. Beavers eat twigs and bark.

Moose and beavers eat tree bark and twigs.

5. Animals with four stomachs are called ruminants. Goats, deer, and cattle have four stomachs. Moose have four stomachs.

Moose, goats, deer, and cattle have four stomachs and are called ruminants.

6. When the snow is deep, a moose will bite off a mouthful of bark. It will chew the bark. Then it will swallow it.

When the snow is deep, a moose will bite off, chew, and swallow a mouthful of bark.

7. Moose flies are pests that bug moose during the summer. During the same time, blackflies and deerflies bother moose.

Moose flies, blackflies, and deerflies are pests that bug moose during the summer.

8. A moose can swim fast. A moose can run about 30 miles an hour.

A moose can swim fast and run about 30 miles an hour.

9. Streams are good places to see moose. You can also see them in ponds and meadows.

Streams, ponds, and meadows are good places to see moose.

10. An angry moose will charge you if it feels threatened. It could kick you. It could bite.

An angry moose will charge, kick, or bite you if it feels threatened.

Next Step Look at a young child's storybook or picture book. See how many of its short sentences you can combine by creating compound subjects or verbs.

Sentence Combining with Compound and Complex Sentences

Ideas from two short sentences can be combined into a compound sentence or a complex sentence. A compound sentence is made up of two simple sentences joined by a comma and a coordinate conjunction (*and, but, or, nor, for, so, yet*) or by a semicolon.

A complex sentence is made up of one simple sentence (independent clause) and one or more subordinate clauses (dependent clauses). A subordinate clause may be introduced by a relative pronoun (*who, which, that, what,* etc.) or by a subordinating conjunction (*after, although, as, because,* etc.). (Refer to 445.2, 456.4, and page 96 in *Write Source 2000* for more information.)

EXAMPLES

Two Simple Sentences:
Many people play sports. Only the best athletes play professional sports.

One Compound Sentence:
Many people play sports, but only the best athletes play professional sports.

Two Simple Sentences:
Successful athletes talk to many people. They often inspire others.

One Complex Sentence:
Because successful athletes talk to many people, they often inspire others.

Directions **Identify each of the following sentences as *compound* or *complex*. Then underline the independent clause (simple sentence) in each sentence. Remember, compound sentences have two independent clauses. (*Note:* If you are unsure whether a word is a subordinate conjunction or not, you can look it up in a dictionary.)**

complex **1.** Once you learn to quit, it becomes a habit.
—Vince Lombardi *(football coach)*

complex **2.** Before you can win a game, you have to not lose it.
—Chuck Noll *(football coach)*

complex **3.** If you can believe it, the mind can achieve it.
—Ronnie Lott *(football player)*

compound **4.** It's not the size of the dog in the fight, but it's the size of the fight in the dog. —Archie Griffin *(football player)*

compound **5.** Winners never quit, and quitters never win. —Unknown

complex **6.** As long as the mind can envision the fact that you can do something, you can do it.
—Arnold Schwarzenegger *(bodybuilder / actor)*

compound **7.** You show me a guy who's afraid to look bad, and I'll show you a guy you can beat every time.
—Lou Brock *(baseball player)*

compound **8.** Everyone has limits on the time he can devote to exercise, and cross-training simply gives you the best return on your investment. —Paula Newby-Fraser *(triathlete)*

compound **9.** Other people may not have had high expectations for me, but I had high expectations for myself.
—Shannon Miller *(gymnast)*

complex **10.** When anyone tells me I can't do anything, I'm just not listening anymore.
—Florence Griffith Joyner *(track athlete)*

complex **11.** Whether I was in a slump or feeling badly or having trouble off the field, the only thing to do was keep swinging. —Hank Aaron *(baseball player)*

compound **12.** It's lack of faith that makes people afraid of meeting challenges, and I believed in myself.
—Muhammad Ali *(boxer)*

complex **13.** If you don't do what's best for your body, you're the one who comes up on the short end.
—Julius Erving *(basketball player)*

compound **14.** You need to play with supreme confidence, or else you'll lose again, and then losing becomes a habit.
—Joe Paterno *(football coach)*

Next Step Write eight short sentences about something you have accomplished. Then combine the sentences into two compound sentences and two complex sentences.

Sentence-Combining Review 1

Two important practices must be established before sentence combining can have a significant effect on your writing. These practices are reading and writing on a regular basis. If you commit yourself to doing that, you'll find sentence combining will begin making a difference in the way you compose. (Turn to pages 93-96 in *Write Source 2000* for more information.)

EXAMPLE

Simple Sentences:
Earl's father is taking a leave of absence. He has taught for 15 years. He teaches in a college. He will be writing a book.

Combined Sentence:
Earl's father, who has taught for 15 years in a college, is taking a leave of absence to write a book.

Directions **Combine each set of simple sentences into longer, smoother-reading ones. Make use of all of the combining techniques you have previously worked on. The first one has been done for you.**

1. The books were scattered.
The books were for a science report.
Magazines were also scattered.
The magazines were for a science report.
The books and magazines were scattered on Kim's desk.

The books and magazines, which were scattered on Kim's desk, were for a science report.

2. The cafeteria was filled with laughter.
The laughter was from students.
The students were telling jokes.
They were telling elephant jokes.

The cafeteria was filled with the laughter of students telling elephant jokes.

3. Fernando found the right kind of film.
The film was for his 35-mm camera.

Fernando found the right kind of film for his 35-mm camera.

4. Fernando walked toward the checkout counter.
He noticed a poorly dressed man.
The man was standing next to a rack of candy bars.

As Fernando walked toward the checkout counter, he noticed a poorly dressed man standing next to a rack of candy bars.

5. The man carefully put some of the candy bars into his coat pocket.
The man put them into his pocket while pretending to read a magazine.

The man carefully put some of the candy bars into his coat pocket while pretending to read a magazine.

6. Fernando saw him do this. He didn't know what to do.

Fernando saw him do this, but he didn't know what to do.

7. The man obviously was trying to shoplift the candy.
He looked like he was really down on his luck.

The man, who looked like he was really down on his luck, obviously was trying to shoplift the candy.

8. Fernando moved toward the checkout counter.
A security guard came down the aisle.

As Fernando moved toward the checkout counter, a security guard came down the aisle.

Next Step Finish the story on your own paper. Exchange stories with a classmate. Find out how your partner developed the unfolding plot. Also note how effectively your partner combined ideas in his or her story.

Sentence-Combining Review 2

Sentences can be combined with phrases, adverb clauses, or adjective clauses. You can use a series of words or phrases, compound subjects, compound verbs, and key words. You can also make complex and compound sentences. (Turn to pages 93-96 in *Write Source 2000* to review sentence-combining methods.)

Directions **In the following passage, combine some of the short sentences into longer, smoother ones. Use as many of the sentence-combining methods as you can. The passage below is a condensed, slightly rewritten version of a scene from *Tom Sawyer* by Mark Twain. (Copy the new sentences on your own paper if necessary.)**

Answers will vary.

Tom appeared on the sidewalk *carrying* ~~He carried~~ a bucket of whitewash *and* ~~He carried~~ a brush with a long handle. Tom looked at the fence *and* all happiness left him. He sighed, ~~He~~ dipped the brush into the whitewash, *and passed it* ~~It passed~~ over the top plank. He repeated the operation. He did it again and again. Tom's energy did not last. He looked in his pocket *and* ~~He~~ got out his worldly wealth and examined it. There was not much there, *at least* ~~There was~~ not enough to pay another boy to paint the fence. It was a dark and hopeless moment, *but then a great, magnificent* ~~An~~ idea burst upon him! ~~It was a great, magnificent idea.~~

He took up his brush and went to work. Ben Rogers came in sight, ~~He was~~ eating an apple. He drew near, *slowed down, and* ~~He slowed down. He~~ stepped into the middle of the street. Tom went on whitewashing. looking at the fence ~~Tom looked at the fence. He looked at it~~ with the eye of an artist. Ben stared a moment. and ~~He~~ ranged up alongside Tom. Tom's mouth watered for the apple. but He stuck to his work. The brush continued to move. Ben watched every move. and ~~He~~ was more and more interested. He said he would give Tom his apple if he could paint the fence. ~~He asked if he could paint the fence. He said he would give Tom his apple.~~ Tom gave up the brush. Ben worked and sweated in the sun. while Tom sat on a barrel and munched the apple.

Ben became tired. so Tom traded the next chance to Billy Fisher for a kite. When Billy Fisher became tired. Johnny Miller bought in for a dead rat and a string to swing it with. By The middle of the afternoon ~~came.~~ Tom was rolling in wealth. ~~He had~~ twelve marbles. ~~He had~~ a tin soldier. ~~He had~~ a dog collar. and ~~He had~~ the handle of a knife. He had had a nice idle time. and The fence had three coats of whitewash on it. He ran out of whitewash. or ~~If he had had more whitewash,~~ he would have bankrupted every boy in the village.

Next Step Read chapter 2 of *Tom Sawyer*. See how your combined sentences match up to Mark Twain's sentences.

Sentence Fragments 1

A sentence fragment may look and sound like a sentence, but it isn't. It is a group of words that is missing either a subject or a verb or that doesn't express a complete thought. (Turn to page 86 in *Write Source 2000* for examples of this type of sentence error.)

EXAMPLE

Sentence Fragment:
Also commonly referred to as seas.

Corrected Sentence:
Oceans are also commonly referred to as seas.
(A subject and a predicate have been added to make this a sentence.)

Directions **Some of the following groups of words are sentences, and some are not. Write an *S* on the line before each sentence; write an *F* before each fragment. Correct the fragments.**

F 1. Oceans cover ~~Covering~~ more than 70 percent of the world's surface.

S 2. Oceans maintain the earth's climate by regulating air temperature.

F 3. Oceans supply ~~Supplying~~ moisture for rain.

F 4. The Pacific Ocean, is by far the largest individual ocean.

S 5. The Pacific covers nearly a third of the earth's surface.

S 6. It is also the deepest ocean, with an average depth of 12,900 feet.

F 7. Every natural element is found in the water of the oceans.

F 8. Evaporation, ~~which~~ removes freshwater from the oceans, leaving the salt behind.

S 9. Rain returns freshwater to the oceans.

F 10. Currents run~~ning~~ through the seas like giant rivers.

 All Write pp. 50 and 368-369

Directions **Write an *S* above each sentence and an *F* above each fragment. Correct each fragment by joining it to the complete sentence or by adding what it needs to be a sentence on its own. The first one has been done for you.**

S F
1. New York is one of the oldest states. A long, interesting history.

New York is one of the oldest states, so it has a long, interesting history.

S F
2. Large groups of Native Americans lived there before white settlers arrived. Including the Algonquians and the Iroquois.

Large groups of Native Americans, including the Algonquians and the Iroquois, lived there before white settlers arrived.

F S
3. Sometime in the year 1624. Thirty families settled in New York.

Sometime in the year 1624, thirty families settled in New York.

Or . . . Thirty families settled in New York sometime in the year 1624.

S F
4. Manhattan was called New Amsterdam. Because it was settled by the Dutch.

Manhattan was called New Amsterdam because it was settled by the Dutch.

F S
5. During the Revolutionary War. More than 30,000 people loyal to the British left New York.

During the Revolutionary War, more than 30,000 people loyal to the British left New York.

S F
6. New York was the 11th state to enter the Union. Albany, the capital city.

Albany is the capital city of New York, which was the 11th state to enter the Union.

Next Step Exchange your work on sentence fragments with a classmate. Discuss any differences in each other's answers.

Sentence Fragments 2

A sentence fragment is not a complete sentence. This group of words may look like a sentence, but it is missing a subject or a verb or is an incomplete thought. (Turn to page 86 in *Write Source 2000*.)

EXAMPLES

Sentence Fragment: **Slept curled up on the rug.** (no subject)
Complete Sentence: **The dog slept curled up on the rug.** (A subject is added.)

Sentence Fragment: **The crow sitting in the tree.** (no verb)
Complete Sentence: **The crow sitting in the tree squawked.** (A verb is added.)

Sentence Fragment: **Not a good idea.** (no subject or verb)
Complete Sentence: **Pulling a dog's tail is not a good idea.** (A subject and a verb are added.)

Directions **On the lines provided, write an *S* if the fragment needs a subject, a *V* if it needs a verb, or a *B* if it needs both a subject and a verb. Then choose from the list of possible answers in the column at the left to turn the fragment into a sentence.**

Subjects and verbs
Kittens are
Barked
Cats had
Ran
~~**Is tired**~~
The dog
Cats have
Herding dogs

V **1.** The dog running after the stick ^is tired^.

S **2.** ^The dog^ Chased a flying disk through the yard.

V **3.** Across the field and around the birdhouse, the crazy cat ^ran^.

S **4.** ^Herding dogs^ Find and herd cattle and sheep out in fields.

B **5.** ^Cats have^ Good hearing, a keen sense of smell, and great night vision.

B **6.** ^Kittens are^ Born blind, deaf, and helpless.

V **7.** After hearing the strange noise, the dog ^barked^.

B **8.** ^Cats had^ Their pictures on ancient Greek coins.

All Write pp. 50 and 368-369

Directions **Each would-be sentence below does not express a complete thought. Add words or phrases so that these fragments become complete sentences. (Rewrite the sentences on the line if necessary.)** *Answers will vary.*

live
1. Dogs and cats in the same household.

smart people
2. People who like dogs are.

I wonder
3. Why dogs howl at the moon.

walking him may be difficult
4. Unless the dog is trained to heel.

are always together
5. Our cat and her toy mouse.

they need to have a curfew
6. Because cats would stay out all night.

7. Which is probably why a dog scratches its ears.

   Dogs often have fleas, which is probably why a dog scratches its ears.

8. Where most house cats enjoy hanging out.

   The bed or a big, soft chair is where most house cats enjoy hanging out.

are wonderful with kids
9. The dog and her puppies.

Next Step Next time you are with a group of people, listen to them talk. See if they use more complete sentences or more sentence fragments when they speak.

Comma Splices

A comma splice happens when two sentences are connected with only a comma. They should be joined with a comma and a coordinating conjunction (*and, but or, nor, for, so, yet*), joined by a semicolon or made into two separate sentences. (Turn to page 86 in *Write Source 2000* for more information.)

EXAMPLE

Comma Splice:

Eating healthy food is good, sometimes you just crave junk food.

Correct:

Eating healthy food is good, but sometimes you just crave junk food.

Directions **Fix each comma splice by adding a connecting word (*and, but, or, nor, for, so, yet*), replacing the comma with a semicolon, or by breaking the sentence into two sentences. The first one has been done for you.** *Answers will vary.*

1. Many foods that are labeled "natural" are full of sugar and salt, *and* some "low-fat" foods have unhealthy ingredients.
2. Air-popped popcorn is fluffy and white; movie-theater popcorn is soggy and yellow.
3. Candy bars taste better than energy bars, *yet* both kinds of bars give you an energy boost.
4. There are regular, no-fat, and low-fat potato chips, *but* the tastiest potato chips are flavored with barbeque, sour cream, and onions.
5. Flour is the main ingredient in bread, rolls, and English muffins. It is also a major ingredient in cakes, donuts, and pies.
6. Some people think pizza is a fattening food, *and* it definitely can be.

Run-Ons

A run-on sentence happens when two sentences run together without punctuation or without a comma and a connecting word (coordinating conjunction). (Turn to page 87 in *Write Source 2000* for more information.)

EXAMPLE

Run-On Sentence:
My grandfather ate unhealthy foods all of his life he lived to be 91.

Corrected Sentence:
My grandfather ate unhealthy foods all of his life, but he lived to be 91.

Directions **Correct each run-on sentence below by making it into either two sentences (add end punctuation) or one sentence (add a semicolon or add a comma and a coordinating conjunction). Try to correct at least half of the run-ons by adding a comma and a coordinating conjunction. The first one has been done for you.**

1. Corn syrup is found in soft drinks and candy bars[, and] it is high in calories.
2. There's corn syrup and high-fructose corn syrup[, but] I don't know the difference.
3. I do know that corn syrup contains dextrin, maltose, and dextrose[, and] I also know that corn syrup comes from the hydrolysis of cornstarch.
4. Hydrolysis sounds like a chemical process[;] it must be helpful.
5. I'm still not sure what corn syrup is[.] I don't know anything about dextrin.
6. Corn syrup tastes good[, and] it is sometimes cheaper to use than regular sugar.
7. I know what is in "100 percent fruit juice[.]" [M]maybe that's what I will drink.
8. My brother drinks only bottled water[.] [H]he says it has no additives.

Next Step Write several sentences about the ingredients in one of your favorite snack foods or desserts. Don't use any punctuation marks or connecting words. Have a friend do the same thing. Exchange papers and correct each other's run-on sentences.

All Write pp. 50 and 399

Comma Splices and Run-Ons

A comma splice is an error made when a writer connects two simple sentences with only a comma. A run-on sentence occurs when two simple sentences run together without any punctuation marks and/or connecting words. (Turn to pages 86 - 87 in *Write Source 2000* for more information and examples.)

EXAMPLES

Comma Splice:
The day is going to be very hot, I like hot weather.
(Two complete thoughts are "spliced" together with only a comma.)

Corrected Sentence:
The day is going to be very hot, but I like hot weather.
(Adding the coordinate conjunction *but* after the comma turns this into a compound sentence.)

Run-On Sentence:
The day was to be the hottest of the summer we decided to get up early.
(Two complete thoughts are incorrectly run together.)

Corrected Sentence:
The day was to be the hottest of the summer; we decided to get up early.
(Adding a semicolon corrects the run-on error.)

Directions **Place a *CS* in front of each comma splice, an *RO* in front of each run-on sentence, and a *C* in front of each correct sentence. Then correct each faulty sentence.** *Answers will vary.*

C 1. The forecast sounded a warning of very high temperatures.

CS 2. Still, it looked like a great day for swimming, [and] we headed for the beach.

RO 3. By noon the heat was intense[, so] we needed to come in out of the sun.

CS 4. It was the perfect time to go for a ride in our air-conditioned car, [and] we decided to look for an ice-cream stand.

C 5. My mother loves the cooler temperatures air-conditioning produces.

CS 6. The searing afternoon sun seemed ready to scorch everything in sight, we had come prepared with three bottles of sunscreen. (correction: sight. We)

RO 7. I didn't want to get a sunburn I remembered the pain that I had experienced the last time it happened. (correction: sunburn; I)

RO 8. We all brought along our beach hats the cool breeze from the water also kept us from overheating. (correction: hats, and the)

RO 9. We had played it smart we were very happy about that fact. (correction: smart, and we)

C 10. Meanwhile, my brother, sweaty from mowing the lawn, complained loudly about the heat.

CS 11. My brother says sledding is more fun than anything, I say water slides are better. (correction: anything. I)

RO 12. There are usually only a few good days for sledding the water slide is open all summer. (correction: sledding, but the)

C 13. Anyway, I think it is ridiculous to think about sledding on a 90° day.

RO 14. When it's hot, I think about swimming that's all I think about. (correction: swimming; that's)

CS 15. I don't like to go to the pool, the beach is more fun. (correction: pool. The)

C 16. I'd spend every day at the beach if I could.

CS 17. It is sure to be hot again, we can count on that. (correction: again, and we)

RO 18. I never complain about the weather I just enjoy it. (correction: weather; I)

C 19. After all, we can't change the weather.

Next Step Design a concrete poem for a *comma splice* or a *run-on sentence.* (Refer to your handbook for an example of concrete poetry.)

Eliminating Wordy Sentences

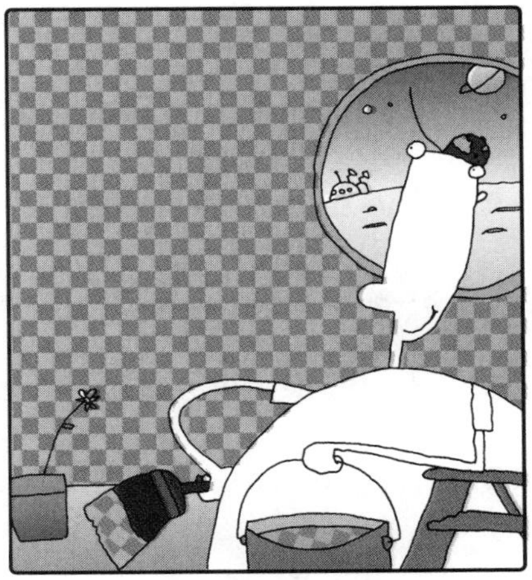

Resist the temptation to pad your writing with words and phrases that add nothing to the point you are trying to make. Also avoid expressions that sound good but seldom add anything worthwhile. (See the example below and on page 87 in *Write Source 2000.*)

EXAMPLE

Incorrect Sentence:
The former tenant who had lived in the apartment before we moved in had painted all the walls with a coat of pink paint.

Correct Sentence:
The former tenant had painted all the walls pink.

Directions **Make the following sentences clearer. Cross out any unnecessary words or phrases. (Read carefully. Some sentences may sound fine at first even though they repeat ideas unnecessarily.) The first sentence has been done for you.** *Answers may vary.*

1. ~~As a general rule,~~ M most of the new submarines ~~that were just purchased~~ are atomic powered.

2. The ~~canceled~~ (optional) flight has been rescheduled for 5:15 p.m. tomorrow ~~evening.~~

3. He arrived ~~there~~ in Terre Haute yesterday morning at 7:00 ~~a.m.~~ and told us a humorous story about his trip ~~that was very funny.~~

4. The ~~very fast~~ race car lapped all of the other cars ~~that were in the race~~ and made it look ~~as if it were~~ easy ~~to do.~~

5. ~~There are~~ F five people ~~who~~ want to drive ~~in their cars~~ to Sarah's house after the movie ~~is over.~~

6. The ~~difficult~~ math problem, which was not easy to understand, caused me to fail the math test ~~with an *F*.~~

All Write pp. 50 and 53

7. The crowded shopping mall, ~~which was filled to the brim with people~~, was evacuated at exactly 8:15 p.m. ~~sharp~~.

8. The detective failed to solve the case because he didn't look for clues ~~or spend time studying things~~ at the scene of the crime.

9. He usually spends about two hours ~~of his time~~ each day at his computer.

10. Despite the strong effort of our team ~~to defeat the opponent and win the game,~~ we came up short and ~~just barely~~ lost.

11. My brother ~~he~~ is taking bowling lessons ~~at the bowling alley~~ while my sister ~~she~~ is practicing ~~her~~ gymnastic routines.

12. In September, my favorite rock group will return ~~again here~~ to ~~repeat their recent performance at~~ Center Stadium.

13. The movie's ~~final~~ ending caught me by surprise ~~because I didn't expect it~~.

14. After we had finished the chores ~~that we worked on~~, my sister and I rushed ~~in a hurry~~ to the theater to see the new movie ~~that was just released~~.

15. The road between Burlington and Elkhorn follows ~~and bends along~~ the ~~winding~~ White River, a river with many twists and turns.

Next Step Write freely and rapidly for 5 to 8 minutes about one of the following subjects (or a subject of your own choosing). Make every effort to write nonstop so that the ideas flow freely.

1. staying at a friend's house
2. the prettiest place I've ever seen
3. a narrow escape from trouble
4. the best pet I ever had

Next, see how wordy your freewriting is. Cross out every word or phrase that is not absolutely necessary. Also have a classmate check your paper for wordy passages.

Rambling Sentences

Just as you should correct any fragments, run-ons, or comma splices in your writing, you also should correct any rambling sentences. Using too many *and*'s or *but*'s could result in a pileup of ideas and confusion for your reader. (Turn to page 87 in *Write Source 2000* for more information.)

Directions

Read the paragraphs below. Look and listen for sentences that ramble. Correct these sentences by taking out some (but not all) of the *and*'s, *but's,* or *so*'s. Then correct the capitalization and punctuation as necessary.

Our student council wanted to help families in need in our community, so we decided to have a canned-goods drive, ~~but~~ to do that, we needed to get students involved on a "massive" scale, and that was no small challenge.

Our adviser, Miss Daniels, thought of starting a friendly competition with each homeroom competing against the other homerooms, ~~and~~ one homeroom at each grade level would win not only recognition in the newspaper but also a pizza party.

Mr. Brzinski's homeroom began the food drive by bringing in the first canned goods, ~~and~~ then Ms. Maher's homeroom got in the act, and before we knew it, all the homerooms were involved, ~~and~~ for the next two weeks, students were mowing lawns and baby-sitting, ~~and~~ buying canned goods, and adding to each homeroom's total. We announced the totals at the end of each day and stacked the cans on the stage in the gymnasium so all of the students could see their homeroom's progress.

To say the least, we were more than pleased with the results, ~~and~~ the newspaper took pictures of the huge piles of cans, ~~and,~~ most importantly, we knew that we had helped many people, and that was the best reward of all.

Editing for Smoothness and Clarity

Transitions or linking words such as "finally," "besides," "however," and "also" are used to connect ideas within or between sentences. In a long or complicated passage, transitions can also map out a pattern or structure for the reader to follow. (Refer to page 106 in your *Write Source 2000* handbook for a list of transitions.)

Directions **Use the following transitions to fill in the blanks in the paragraph below. (*Note:* Some transition words should be followed by commas.) The first one has been done for you.**

as soon as	**finally**	**before**
whenever	**in addition**	**in fact**

My mother really dislikes computers. ___In fact,___ she often says she wishes those "horrible machines" had never been invented. My mother shows her dislike and what actually seems to be fear in several different ways. ___Before___ she even sits down at the computer, she approaches it as you would a dangerous animal that might attack at any moment. ___As soon as___ her hands touch the keyboard, she yanks them back as though she had been bitten.

She shows her mistrust in other ways as well. ___Whenever___ she saves any material, she stares at the screen the same way someone would look down into a well where something very valuable had been dropped. ___In addition,___ she claims that the computer is "stealing" instead of saving. ___Finally,___ my mother is convinced that the mouse is alive and moves wherever it feels like moving regardless of where she wants it to go.

Next Step In a well-written paragraph, explain your own feelings about computers. Use transition words to aid in clarifying your ideas.

Sentence Errors 1

It is important to present your ideas in clear, complete sentences. Sometimes errors appear in writing that make ideas hard to understand. Some of these errors are **sentence fragments, run-on sentences,** and **comma splices.** These sentence errors are easy to fix. (See the examples below and on pages 86-87 in *Write Source 2000* for more information.)

EXAMPLES

Fragment: **If it leaked.**	*Complete:* **If it leaked, it would sink.**
Run-On **It leaked it sank.**	*Complete:* **It leaked; it sank.**
Comma Splice: **It leaked, it sank.**	*Complete:* **It leaked. It sank.**

Directions **Write *C* in front of a sentence that is correct, *CS* in front of a comma splice, *RO* in front of a run-on sentence, and *SF* in front of a sentence fragment. (The fragment example may also contain a complete sentence.) Then fix the sentence errors. One sentence will need two corrections. The first one has been done for you.**

__SF__ **1.** The movie *Titanic* tells the story of the disaster. As seen by one survivor.

__SF__ **2.** Survivor Dr. Washington Dodge of San Francisco reported his observations of the wreck. Giving details in a 1912 newspaper story.

__CS__ **3.** We had retired to our stateroom, the noise of the collision was not at all alarming.

__RO__ **4.** They started to lower the lifeboats after a lapse of some minutes there was little excitement.

CS 5. The passengers were constantly being assured that there was no danger, as a matter of extra precaution, the women and children were placed in the lifeboats.

RO 6. I believe there were 20 boats lowered away all together the excitement began after the sixth or seventh boat was launched.

C 7. Some of the passengers fought with such desperation to get into the lifeboats that the officers threatened to shoot them.

CS 8. The starboard side of the *Titanic* struck the big berg, the ice soon piled up on the deck.

C 9. None of us had the slightest realization that the ship had received its death wound.

CS 10. Mrs. Isidor Straus showed most admirable courage, she refused to leave her husband even though she was urged to get into a boat.

RO 11. The 13th boat was filled with 20 or 30 children and a few women everyone was trying to stay calm.

CS 12. When the boats were drawing away from the ship, people could hear the orchestra playing "Lead, Kindly Light," rockets were going up from the *Titanic* in the wonderfully clear night, heroic husbands and fathers were waving and throwing kisses to their womenfolk in the receding lifeboats.

Next Step Write a short paragraph about the *Titanic* or another tragedy you've heard or read about. As you write, do not put any punctuation marks or capital letters in any of the sentences. Exchange papers with a classmate; then go back and insert the punctuation marks and capital letters where they belong.

Sentence Errors 2

It is important to present your ideas in clear, concise sentences. Sometimes ideas are hard to understand because the sentences are wordy or ramble on. Try to avoid these kinds of sentences by writing about just one idea in each sentence and by eliminating extra words, especially *and*'s. Also avoid using too many short, choppy sentences. Combine them into smoother, more detailed sentences to make your writing clearer and easier to read. (Review pages 87 and 93-96 in *Write Source 2000.*)

Directions

Improve the following sentences by fixing rambling sentences, eliminating wordiness, and combining sentences. (*Note:* There are many acceptable ways to do this.) The first sentence has been done for you.

Answers will vary.

The sinking of the *Titanic* was one of the worst sea disasters ~~that happened at sea~~ in history. The ~~luxurious~~ British luxury liner left England on its first voyage across the Atlantic, and two days later the ship struck an iceberg and sank. ~~and~~ About 1,500 people died.

Work on the *Titanic* started with 15,000 workers in March 1909 and ~~work~~ was completed on the ship's outside in May 1911. It took ~~another~~ 10 more months to finish the interiors of the ship and to add boilers, engines, and four funnels. Only the first three funnels were real. The fourth funnel was ~~a fake funnel~~ added to make the ship look like it was larger and faster.

The *Titanic* was sailing ~~across the Atlantic Ocean on its way~~ to New York City when it struck an iceberg just before midnight on April 14, 1912. The ship sank in less than three hours. The *Titanic* was thought to be unsinkable ~~and many people believed it would not sink~~ because it had 16 watertight compartments, but the iceberg punctured 5 or 6 of them. The

All Write pp. 50 and 56-58

walls in the watertight compartments went only about halfway up the ship's hull. ~~and~~ Water poured into the compartments, ~~and the water flowed into the next compartment and it filled them up~~ like water filling the compartments in an ice-cube tray.

There were a number of reasons for the disaster. The ship had been sailing too fast in dangerous waters, ~~and~~ there were not enough lifeboats for all the people, and a nearby ship did not come to the rescue because its radio was not on. The night of April 14 was clear, and the water was calm. ~~and the calm water made no waves and~~ That made the iceberg difficult to see until it was too late.

Believe it or not, the *Titanic* carried more lifeboats than was required by law ~~at the time~~ in 1912. The *Titanic* was equipped with a total of 20 lifeboats that could carry ~~a total of only around~~ about 1,200 people. Many people refused to get in the lifeboats because they thought the *Titanic* ~~passenger ship~~ was safe from sinking ~~to the bottom of the sea and~~. As a result, the lifeboats went away with only about 650 people in them.

Next Step Read a newspaper article and look at the sentences. There will probably be few rambling or wordy sentences, but the sentence types and lengths may be similar. See if you can rewrite some of the sentences so they are more varied.

Sentence Parts

Our language alarm system can detect faulty sentences just by listening. If someone said, “Clumsy plays Jack a tuba looking,” our response would be “Say what?” We know that sentences should clearly show someone doing something, as in “Jack plays a clumsy-looking tuba.”

EXAMPLE

Scrambled Sentence:
Slipping back to their holes a couple of night crawlers we spotted.

Unscrambled Sentence:
We spotted a couple of night crawlers slipping back to their holes.

Directions **In the following activity, arrange the scrambled sentence parts so they express thoughts that make good sense. Make sure to add the necessary capital letters and punctuation marks. (The starred word groups should be at the beginning of each of your unscrambled sentences.)**

1. with my sister and me
and turned on the TV
I went into the living room
knowing my mom was a little angry*

Knowing my mom was a little angry with my sister and me, I went into the living room and turned on the TV.

2. a horror movie
it gave me*
alone in my room
with the light off
the feeling of watching

It gave me the feeling of watching a horror movie alone in my room with the light off.

3. out for drama
I no longer
with boys on campus*
for the male roles
when I went
got recruited

— from *Me Me Me Me Me* by M. E. Kerr

With boys on campus, I no longer got recruited for the male roles when I went out for drama.

4. to the cows
hanging their lanterns*
my uncle and my cousins
from convenient pegs
and distributed the morning feedings
took hayforks

— from *Rascal* by Sterling North

Hanging their lanterns from convenient pegs, my uncle and my cousins took hayforks and distributed the morning feedings to the cows.

5. cross-legged
rolling her five marbles
she sat*
between her palms
on the bed

— from *The Marble Champ* by Gary Soto

She sat cross-legged on the bed, rolling her five marbles between her palms.

Next Step Make sure you compare your results with the results of one or more of your classmates. There might be more than one way to organize the parts into effective sentences.

Find three or more smooth-reading or eye-opening sentences in a favorite book or magazine. Then scramble the important parts in each of these sentences. Exchange work and arrange your classmate's lists of parts into meaningful sentences. Compare your creations with the originals.

Adding Style to Your Sentences

One of the easiest ways to add style and variety to writing is to use modifiers, phrases, and clauses at the beginnings of your sentences. If too many of your sentences start the same way—with the subject—your writing may begin to sound dull or flat.

Directions **Each of the following sentences begins with a subject. Reword each sentence twice (use two different beginnings). You can use one-word modifiers, phrases, or clauses to start your revised sentences. (The subject in each sentence is highlighted in boldfaced type.) The first one has been done for you.**

1. **Treasures** totaling billions of dollars are waiting across the United States for treasure hunters.

a. *Across the United States, treasures totaling billions of dollars are waiting for treasure hunters.*

b. *Waiting for treasure hunters across the United States are treasures totaling billions of dollars.*

2. **Gold mines,** overgrown and hidden by time, contain large fortunes in the western part of our country.

a. *Overgrown and hidden by time, gold mines in the western part of our country contain large fortunes.*

b. *In the western part of our country, gold mines, overgrown and hidden by time, contain large fortunes.*

All Write p. 45

3. **People** distrustful of banks hid valuables that now remain unclaimed.

a. *Distrustful of banks, people hid valuables that now remain unclaimed.*

b. *Some valuables that now remain unclaimed were hidden by people distrustful of banks.*

4. Treasure **hunters** searching for hot prospects read old newspapers and magazines while the rest of us work regular jobs.

a. *While the rest of us work regular jobs, treasure hunters search for hot prospects by reading old newspapers and magazines.*

b. *Searching for hot prospects, treasure hunters read old newspapers and magazines while the rest of us work regular jobs.*

5. Antique **dolls,** in addition to antique furniture, plates, and jewelry, are very valuable today because many people collect old and interesting objects.

a. *In addition to antique furniture, plates, and jewelry, antique dolls are very valuable today because many people collect old and interesting objects.*

b. *Because many people collect old and interesting objects, antique dolls, in addition to antique furniture, plates, and jewelry, are very valuable today.*

6. The **tool** most valuable to a treasure hunter is his or her own mind, even though a good metal detector can come in handy.

a. *Though a good metal detector can come in handy, the tool most valuable to a treasure hunter is his or her own mind.*

b. *To a treasure hunter, the most valuable tool is his or her own mind, though a good metal detector can come in handy.*

Sentence Expanding

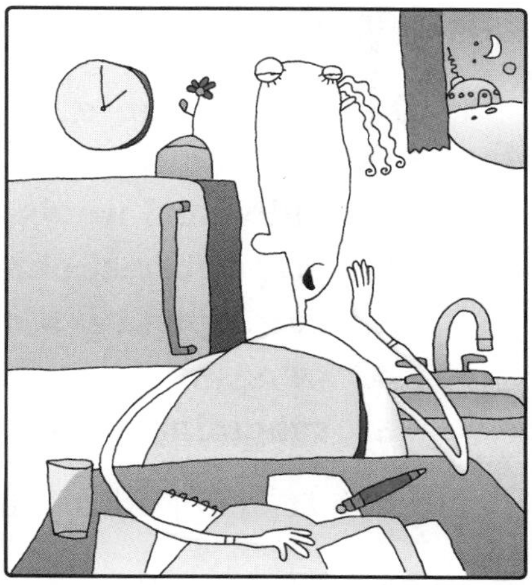

What is it that keeps you reading a novel until midnight or trying to figure out *whodunit* in the latest movie thriller? It's the tantalizing details doled out in bits and pieces. Unpredictable, scary, or vivid—details make a story better.

Details often spill out of a writer's mind spontaneously. The writer might start with a brief sentence, attach a detail to it, tweak the wording a bit, tack on another detail, and so on. This is called **sentence expanding.** It allows a writer to be playful and vivid. Read the following examples and then try the exercise.

EXAMPLE

Start with a Basic Sentence:
Julie was studying.

First, we could say *when* Julie was studying:
***Late last night,* Julie was studying.**

Second, we could say *where* Julie was studying:
Late last night, Julie was studying *at the kitchen table.*

Third, we could say *how* Julie was studying:
Late last night, Julie was studying at the kitchen table, *memorizing terms.*

Finally, we could say *why* Julie was studying:
Late last night, Julie was studying at the kitchen table, memorizing terms *for tomorrow's science quiz.*

Special Note: We could add more information, but the sentence as it now stands reads well. The point is to make a smooth-reading, interesting sentence, not a sentence that is piled too high with detail.

Directions

Now you try it. On your own paper, expand the following brief thoughts by adding details. Look for where these details might naturally fit—before, within, or after the basic sentence. (See "The Writer's Corner" on the next page for help.)

1. Roy slipped.
2. Ms. Rogers entered.
3. José swung.
4. Marcia turned.
5. The storm started.
6. A bear growled.

The Writer's Corner

Details come in a variety of shapes and sizes. Try to use the five different forms below when expanding basic sentences:

1. **individual words** (quietly)
2. **prepositional phrases** (at the kitchen table)
3. **participial** (*-ing* or *-ed*) **phrases** (memorizing a list of words)
4. ***who, which,* or *that* clauses** (who needed an *A*)
5. **subordinate clauses** (because the semester was almost over)

Let's try expanding the sentence "Roy slipped." How might you get started?

- First, you could say *when* he slipped.

- Second, you could say *where* he slipped.

- Third, you could say *how* he slipped.

- Fourth, you could say *why* he slipped. (This fourth element is optional. If your sentence already says enough, leave it alone.)

Next Step For more practice, write five of your own basic sentences. Then exchange them with a classmate and produce interesting expanded sentences from your partner's list. Compare your work with your classmate's. Make note of sentences you especially like in each other's work.

Language Activities

Every activity includes a main practice section in which you learn about or review the different parts of speech. Most of the activities include helpful handbook references. In addition, the **Next Step** activities give you follow-up practice with certain skills.

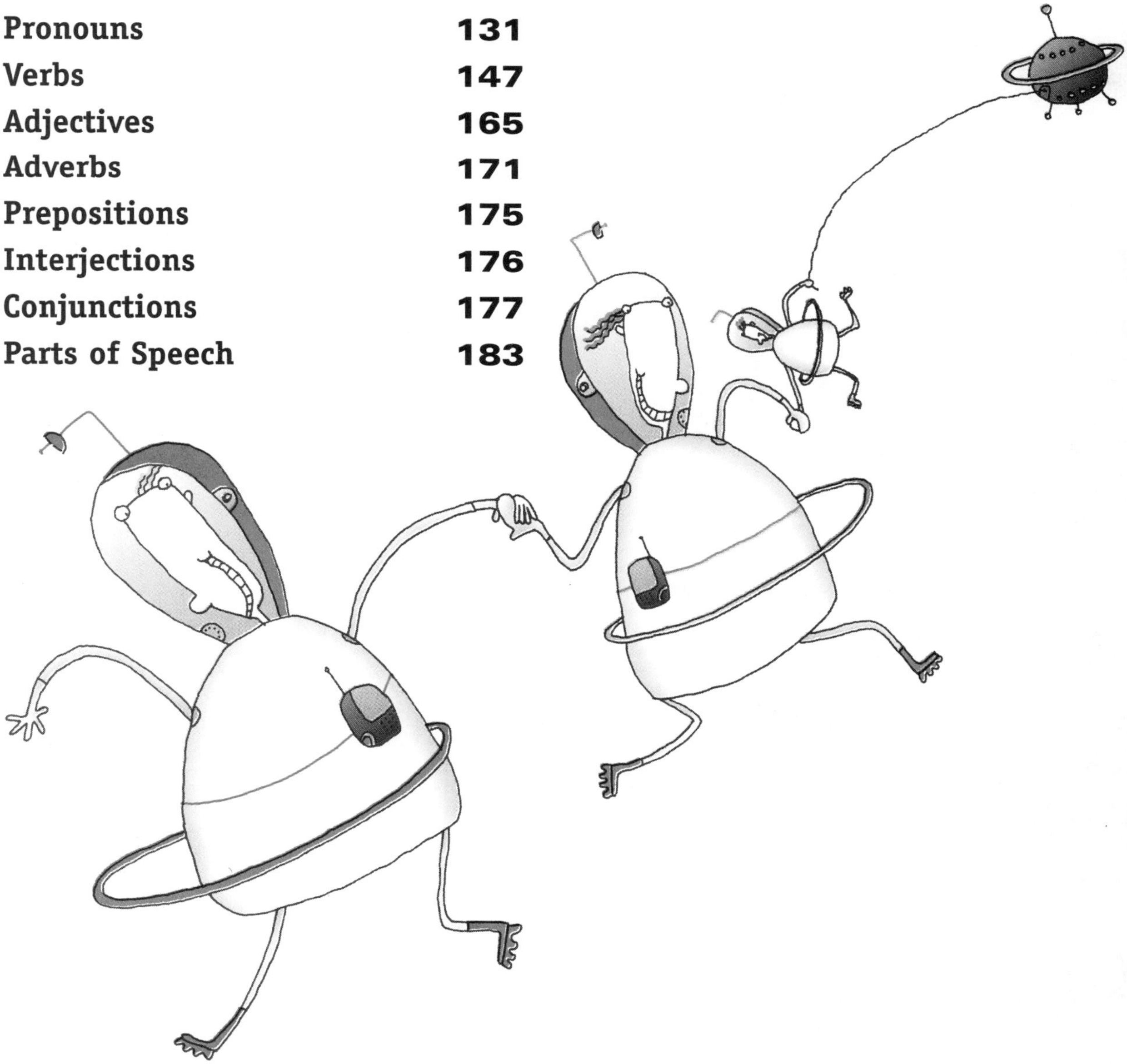

Uses of Nouns

A noun can be the subject of a sentence, or it can be part of the predicate of a sentence. It can be possessive or can act as an object. (Turn to 440.5-441.3 in *Write Source 2000* for more information.)

EXAMPLES

Subject Noun:
A subject noun is the subject, the doer, or the noun being talked about in the sentence.
The *fish* jumped out of the lake.

Predicate Noun:
A predicate noun follows a form of the verb *be* (*is, are, was, were*) and renames the subject.
Swimming is a fun summertime *activity*.

Possessive Noun:
A possessive noun shows possession and contains an apostrophe.
The *boat's* engine stopped, so the fisher had to paddle back.

Object Nouns:
The volleyball game was played in the *sand*.
- *Object of a Preposition:* The noun *sand* is an object of the preposition *in*.

The setter bumped the *ball*.
- *Direct Object:* The noun *ball* is a direct object, which receives the action directly from the subject *setter*.

The setter gave the *spiker* a good set.
- *Indirect Object:* The noun *spiker* is an indirect object, which indirectly receives the action. To have an indirect object in a sentence, there also must be a direct object.

Directions **For each underlined noun, write an *S* if it is the subject of the sentence, a *PN* if it is a predicate noun, a *POS* if it is a possessive noun, or an *O* if it is an object noun. The first one has been done for you.**

PN **1.** Summer is the best time for outdoor activities such as swimming and volleyball.

S **2.** Swimming in a lake is different from swimming in a pool.

O 3. When swimming in a lake, you have to share the water [DO] with boaters, jet skiers, and people who fish.

O 4. When swimming in a pool on a hot summer day [OP], you may find yourself sharing the water with the entire neighborhood.

POS 5. A swimming pool's water temperature is usually warmer than a lake's.

S 6. Too many bodies in a pool make the water even warmer.

O 7. Swim goggles protect your eyes [DO] from the chlorine in a pool.

O 8. In a lake, you can wear a mask [DO], fins, and a snorkel to see underwater.

PN 9. Lifeguards at a pool or beach must be excellent swimmers.

O 10. They may have to give an injured swimmer [IO] first aid.

PN 11. After a refreshing swim, a sandy beach is a great place to play volleyball.

PN 12. Volleyball played with two people on each team is a fast-paced game.

O 13. It provides each team member [IO] plenty of exercise.

POS 14. A team's success depends on how well the two players work together.

O 15. Each team usually uses all three hits [DO] to return a serve.

S 16. One player hits the ball high, so the second player can get under it.

O 17. The second player then sets the ball near the net [OP].

O 18. The first player then charges in and spikes the ball [DO].

POS 19. After playing an afternoon's worth of beach volleyball, you can jump back in the lake and cool off.

Next Step Look over the exercise you just completed. In the sentences marked with an *O,* label the underlined nouns as either direct objects (*DO*), indirect objects (*IO*), or objects of prepositions (*OP*). Your handbook can help you to decide which choice is best.

Concrete, Abstract, and Collective Nouns

A noun names either a person, a place, a thing, or an idea. Nouns can be sorted by what they name. A **concrete** noun names something that can be seen or touched. An **abstract** noun names something that you can think about, such as an idea or a feeling, but that you cannot see or touch. A **collective** noun names a collection or group of persons, animals, places, or things. (Turn to 439.3-439.5 in *Write Source 2000*.)

EXAMPLES

Concrete Nouns: **student, cookie, Denmark**
Abstract Nouns: **poverty, courage, quality**
Collective Nouns: **class, batch, team**

Directions **In front of each of the following words, write *C* for concrete noun, *A* for abstract noun, or *COL* for collective noun.**

C	**1.**	brick
A (or) COL	**2.**	pride
COL	**3.**	cluster
COL (or) C	**4.**	Rocky Mountains
C	**5.**	snowboard
A	**6.**	excellence
C	**7.**	computer
COL	**8.**	bunch
COL (or) C	**9.**	family
COL (or) C	**10.**	Green Bay Packers
A	**11.**	happiness
A	**12.**	peace
A	**13.**	fear
C (or) COL	**14.**	herd
C	**15.**	*Titanic*
A	**16.**	democracy
C (or) COL	**17.**	school
C (or) COL	**18.**	United States
C (or) COL	**19.**	flock
A	**20.**	love
C	**21.**	tree
A	**22.**	religion
COL (or) C	**23.**	team
A	**24.**	freedom
C	**25.**	bike
C	**26.**	water
A	**27.**	help
C	**28.**	dog
C	**29.**	pizza
COL (or) C	**30.**	pack
A	**31.**	anger
COL	**32.**	group
C (or) COL	**33.**	litter

Directions **Complete the sentences below, choosing some of your words from the previous list of concrete, abstract, and collective nouns.**

1. My favorite sports team is the ______________________________ .
2. I think our school needs more ______________________________ .
3. ______________________________ is a person I admire.
4. My friends and I could be called a ______________ of ______________ .
5. I would like to visit the ______________________________ .
6. In my ______________ , we have a pet ______________________ .
7. ______________________________ is something that I strongly believe in.
8. I could listen to the music of ______________________________ all day.
9. If I lived on a farm, I would raise a ______________ of ______________ .
10. When I see ______________ , I feel ______________________ .
11. My best vacation was in ______________________________ .
12. In our ______________ , we have a strong sense of ______________ .
13. On television, I like to watch ______________________________ .
14. The emotion that best describes me is ______________________________ .
15. I would like to meet ______________ at the ______________ .

Next Step Everyone has heard of a herd of cows, but do you know what a group of geese is called? List 10 different animals and then see if you can label each one with the correct collective noun. (Check your answers in the handbook.)

Nouns Review

Directions

In the blanks below, list any common nouns that come to mind. (They are the ones that don't begin with capital letters.) But be quick. Try to show off your common k(noun)ledge by filling in the spaces in 3 to 5 minutes. (Turn to 439.2 in *Write Source 2000* for more information.)

Common K(noun)ledge

Get your "word's worth" in a poem.

Directions **Write a list poem for one of the nouns in your list.** **(Turn to page 207 in *Write Source 2000* for an example.)**

Next Step On your own paper, explain what is meant by the following types of nouns: *proper nouns, concrete nouns, abstract nouns,* and *collective nouns.* (Don't look in your handbook.) Then share your explanations with a classmate. Then compare your explanations with those in your handbook.

Pronouns

Pronouns take the place of nouns and help make your writing read smoothly.

EXAMPLE

Without Pronouns:

Tony woke up and thought that Tony would vary Tony's routine and drive Tony's car to work instead of taking the bus.

With Pronouns:

Tony woke up and thought that he would vary his routine and drive his car to work instead of taking the bus.

Directions **There are six kinds of pronouns covered below: *personal, relative, indefinite, interrogative, demonstrative,* and *reflexive.* Turn to 441.4-445.3 in *Write Source 2000*. Then fill in the blanks below.**

1. Personal pronouns take the place of nouns in a sentence.
2. An example of a singular personal pronoun would be I (you, he, she, it, me, him, her).
3. An example of a plural personal pronoun would be we (you, they, us, them).
4. An example of a reflexive pronoun would be myself (himself, herself, itself, yourself, themselves, ourselves).
5. Three examples of relative pronouns would be who, whose, and whom (which, what, that, whoever, whomever, whatever, whichever).
6. Three examples of indefinite pronouns would be all, another, and any (anybody, anyone, anything, both, each, each one, either, everybody, everyone, etc.).
7. An interrogative pronoun asks a question.
8. The four demonstrative pronouns listed in your handbook are this, that, these, and those.

Directions **Underline all of the pronouns in the following selection. Then write the antecedent (the word the pronoun substitutes for) above each pronoun. The first few have been done for you. (*Note:* Indefinite pronouns such as *everything* or *anybody* do not have specific antecedents.)**

Last week Mitch turned 17. After getting permission from his [Mitch's] parents, Mitch bought his [Mitch's] first car. It [Car] was a lime green, 1971 Volkswagen Super Beetle. When he [Mitch] brought it [car] home, his [Mitch's] parents were a bit surprised.

"I [Father] thought you [Mitch] were going to buy a truck," said his [Mitch's] father.

"Well, this [Volkswagen Super Beetle] was cheaper, and I [Mitch] love the color," replied Mitch.

Mitch's father had owned a Beetle when Mitch was a baby, so they [Mitch and Father] decided to fix it [car] up together. They [Mitch and Father] gave it [car] a good tune-up. Then they [Mitch and Father] checked its [car's] seat belts to make sure they [seat belts] were working properly.

"What should we [Father and Mitch] do next?" asked Mitch.

"Since everything is fixed inside, we [Mitch and Father] should wash the outside," said Dad.

So the Beetle, as dirty as city snow in March, was cleaned and polished to a glowing green. With fuzzy, purple dice hanging from the rearview mirror, and with the roads clean and dry on an August day, Mitch took his [Mitch's] car for its [car's] first official spin. He [Mitch] went to the store to get milk for his [Mitch's] mom.

Next Step Read the selection to yourself, using only the antecedents, no pronouns. We think you'll see the need for pronouns here . . . and in your own writing.

Number and Person of Pronouns

When used in a sentence, personal pronouns have both a number and a person. (See 442.2 - 442.5 and the chart on the bottom of page 443 in *Write Source 2000* for more information on the number and person of common pronouns.)

EXAMPLES

Pronoun Number:
A pronoun's number tells how many people or objects it refers to. The number can be either singular or plural. *You, your,* and *yours* may be singular or plural.

I **volunteered to defend Boston from the British.** (singular)

We **were given uniforms and taught to drill.** (plural)

Pronoun Person:
A pronoun's person tells who is making a statement, who is being spoken to, or whom the statement is about. A *first-person pronoun* takes the place of the speaker's name. A *second-person pronoun* refers to the person or thing spoken to. A *third-person pronoun* names the person or thing spoken about.

I **saluted the commanding officer.** (first person)

You **are a fine soldier.** (second person)

He **handed the young recruit a drum.** (third person)

Directions **For each underlined pronoun, write its number and person. Use an *S* for singular number and a *P* for plural. Use a *1* for first person, a *2* for second person, and a *3* for third person. The first sentence has been done for you.**

P-1 **1.** About nine o'clock at night, we marched down to Breed's Hill.

P-3 **2.** The British marched slowly, and they nearly reached our fort when the battle began.

S-1 **3.** This being my first battle, I remember great noise and much confusion.

S-2 **4.** Our sergeant said, "You are young and quick. Run and bring back some medicine."

S-3 **5.** "The major has been hurt, and he needs it quickly."

P-3 **6.** When I returned to the hill, our men were confused, and they were talking about retreat.

S-1 **7.** I stayed with some others and covered the retreat until the British were close at hand.

P-3 **8.** They then took over our fort and four pieces of artillery.

S or P-2 **9.** And to tell you the truth, very few of our reinforcements made it in time.

P-3 **10.** Then our orders came, and they said we were to make the best retreat we could.

P-1 **11.** We were tired, but we ran as fast as we could up Breed's Hill.

S-1 **12.** I was exhausted by the time we reached the top, but we were safe—at least for the moment.

Next Step Without looking at the definitions at the beginning of this activity, write out your own explanation of the "number" and "person" of a pronoun. Use these words: *singular, plural, first person, second person,* and *third person.*

Uses of a Pronoun

In a sentence, a pronoun can be a subject pronoun, an object pronoun, or a possessive pronoun. (For more information about pronouns, turn to 442.6 - 443.2 in *Write Source 2000*.)

EXAMPLES

Subject Pronoun:
A subject pronoun is the subject of the sentence.
After five years, *I* was still in the army.
(The pronoun *I* is a subject pronoun.)

Object Pronoun:
Following an action verb, an object pronoun can be a direct object or an indirect object. It can also be the object of a preposition.

I helped *him* buckle on his sword.
- *Direct Object:* (The pronoun *him* is a direct object.)

I never heard anything but good stories about *him*.
- *Object of the Preposition:* (The pronoun *him* is an object of a preposition.)

Possessive Pronoun:
A possessive pronoun shows ownership.
Meeting the general was one of *my* proudest moments.
(The pronoun *my* is a possessive pronoun.)

Directions **Above each underlined pronoun, write an S if the pronoun is the subject, an *O* if it is an object, or a *P* if it is a possessive.**

We arrived at the camp, and we were very anxious for battle. Night came upon us, and General Morgan joked with his men. The next morning was bitterly cold, and the men slapped their hands together to keep them warm. About sunrise, the British advanced toward our position. They shouted at us, and we yelled back at them. The general galloped by the men and told them not to fire until they could see the whites of their eyes. The British charged at us with bayonets, and we retreated. Just as we got to our horses, their dragoons overtook us. But in a few moments, our calvary attacked them, and they ran off. As both lines of infantry clashed, the general ordered me to capture a British artillery piece. I saluted him and charged with my men. We overran their position, and it was ours.

Now it was our job to use the artillery against them. The problem was that we did not have any ammunition. So we decided the only way we could get the cannonballs we needed was to collect those that had been shot at us earlier.

We found cannonballs everywhere. Some were stuck halfway through tree trunks. Others were buried under piles of rocks. Some were even inside tents while others were mixed in with pots and pans. When our scavenger hunt was over, we had gathered nearly 100 cannonballs. Now all we needed was gunpowder and a target.

Next Step Write a paragraph about an activity that you do with a group (a sports team, a choir, a club). In the paragraph use the pronouns *I, me, my, we, us,* and *our.*

Intensive and Reflexive Pronouns

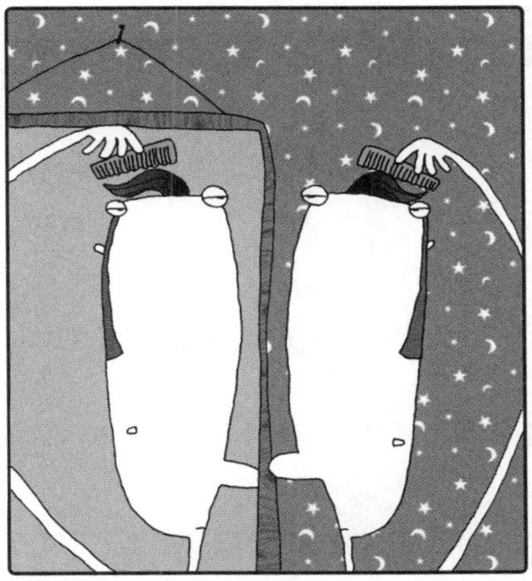

A **reflexive pronoun** acts like a mirror. It reflects back upon the subject of a sentence. An **intensive pronoun** emphasizes or intensifies the noun or pronoun it refers to. Writers use the intensive pronoun as a spotlight to focus attention on the antecedent (the word the intensive pronoun refers to). (Turn to 444.4 - 445.2 in *Write Source 2000* for more information.)

EXAMPLES

Reflexive Pronoun:
The young man looked at *himself* in the mirror.
(The pronoun *himself* reflects back to the antecedent *man*.)

Intensive Pronoun:
She *herself* never carries a mirror.
(The pronoun *herself* emphasizes or intensifies the antecedent *she*. The sentence would still be complete if the intensive pronoun was taken away.)

Directions **On the seven blanks below, write a short sentence for each of the seven reflexive pronouns listed at 445.2 in *Write Source 2000*.**

Reflexive Pronouns

1. ______________________________
2. ______________________________
3. ______________________________
4. ______________________________
5. ______________________________
6. ______________________________
7. ______________________________

Directions **On the following lines, finish the story started below. It's a story about a peacock named Narcissus. In your story, try to use all seven of the pronouns from your handbook (as reflexives or intensives).** ***Hint:*** **See what a dictionary says about Narcissus.**

Once upon a time, there was a peacock who loved to look at himself in the pond near his . . .

Next Step Exchange stories with a classmate. Circle each reflexive or intensive pronoun you find. Label each one *R* for reflexive or *I* for intensive.

Pronouns and Antecedents 1

A pronoun is used in place of a noun. The noun it refers to or replaces is called an **antecedent.** The antecedent usually comes before the pronoun. Pronouns must agree with their antecedents in number, person, and gender. When using pronouns, make sure that each pronoun-antecedent reference is clear, so readers are not confused. (Turn to page 90 and section 441.4 in *Write Source 2000* for more information.)

EXAMPLES

The *detectives* solved the case. *They* found the missing money.
(The plural pronoun *they* refers back to the plural antecedent *detectives.*)

Unclear Pronoun Reference:
The detective cornered the thief. He ran quickly down the alley.
(Who ran, the detective or the thief?)

Clear Pronoun Reference:
The detective cornered the thief, who ran quickly down the alley.
(Changing the pronoun *he* to *who* shows that the thief ran down the alley.)

Directions **Write the antecedent for each underlined pronoun inside the parentheses following it. The first two sentences have been done for you.**

Sam Slade and his (Sam's) partner, Millie Marlowe, were in their office. It was a quiet morning, so they (Sam and Millie) started cleaning up the place. Then the phone rang. Its (phone) loud ring startled the pair.

"I'll (Millie) get it," said Millie as she dashed to the phone on her (Millie's) desk. "It's for you (Sam), Sam."

Sam grabbed the phone and listened carefully for a few minutes.

He hung it (phone) up and sat on the edge of his (Sam's) desk. "We (Sam and Millie) have a case!" he exclaimed. "That was my (Sam's) mom. Someone swiped the chocolate chip cookies and her (Mom's) special secret recipe, the one she (Mom) used for the charity bake sale."

The two detectives hopped on their (detectives') bikes. "Let's rock and roll," yelled Sam.

"Race you (Sam) there. My (Millie's) bike is faster than yours," replied Millie, and off they (Millie and Sam) zoomed.

Millie's bike was faster, and she reached Sam's house first.

Sam's mom was waiting in the kitchen, and she (Mom) showed them (Sam and Millie) a trail of cookie crumbs.

It (Trail) led Sam and Millie to a closet door with a chocolate-smeared handle.

They opened it (door) and looked inside.

There sat the two thieves—Sam's brother, Sid, and Sid's dog, Sherlock—with their (Sid's and Sherlock's) faces stuffed with chocolate chip cookies.

"I have you (Sid and Sherlock) now," said Sam.

Next Step Write your own definition of an "antecedent" without looking up the answer.

Pronouns and Antecedents 2

Directions **In the following sentences, correct any underlined pronoun that does not agree with its antecedent. Also rewrite any sentences to make pronoun-antecedent references clearer. (Turn to page 90 and then section 441.4 in *Write Source 2000* for more information.)**

Sid and Sherlock looked at all the faces looking at them. ~~They~~ *Sam, Millie, and Mom* looked surprised. The two cookie criminals crawled out of the closet. ~~He~~ *They* definitely looked guilty.

"What did you do with ~~her~~ *my* cookies?" asked Mom.

"We were hungry," answered Sid as he held out an empty plate.

His mother took the plate and set ~~them~~ *it* on the counter.

"I was just going to take one, but Sherlock wanted some, too." ~~He~~ *Sherlock* sat and licked chocolate from his mouth.

"It's okay, Sherlock," said Sam, and he walked over to him.

"What happened to the recipe?" asked Millie as Mom put ~~his~~ *her* arm around Sid.

"It's right here," said the boy, and ~~she~~ *he* took it out of ~~her~~ *his* pocket.

"We were going to make more cookies to replace the ones ~~they~~ *we* ate," he said. ~~She~~ *Mom* hugged him and smiled.

All Write pp. 53 and 379

Directions

Sid and Sherlock surprise Mom. They make cookies for her while she is napping. A phone call interrupts them, and Sid has to take down a very complicated message. Write down the message that Sid took for Mom. Be sure that all pronouns agree with their antecedents.

Pronoun Shifts and Double Subjects

Problems with pronouns can lead to confusing sentences. One common problem is a **pronoun shift.** A pronoun shift happens when a pronoun's person does not agree with its antecedent's person. (Turn to page 90 and then sections 442.3 - 442.5 in *Write Source 2000* for more about pronouns and person.)

Another problem to avoid is a **double subject.** This problem occurs whenever you use a pronoun immediately after the subject, which results in two words being used as the subject when you need only one.

EXAMPLES

Pronoun Shift:
If students today complain about school, *you* should learn what schools were like after the Civil War.
(*Students* is a third-person subject, so a third-person pronoun should be used.)
Corrected:
If students today complain about school, *they* should learn what schools were like after the Civil War.

Double Subject:
In the pioneer days, children they were often taught by their parents.
(The word *they* should be taken out.)
Corrected:
In the pioneer days, children were often taught by their parents.

Directions **Correct the pronoun shifts and double subjects in the following sentences by crossing out any incorrect pronouns. Write the correct form of the pronoun above each pronoun-shift error. The first sentence has been done for you.**

1. In the country, a child ~~he~~ could walk several miles to ~~your~~ *his* school.
2. In the first public schools, children ~~they~~ went to school for 16 weeks or less.
3. Many country schools ~~they~~ had only one room for students of all ages.

4. A typical 30-by-35-foot school ~~it~~ held 50 students in one room.

5. In newer city schools, two children shared a bench and a desk, and at exercise time, ~~he~~ *they* flipped up the bench and exercised right by ~~your~~ *their* desks.

6. Children in grades one through eight ~~they~~ exercised with a wand. The students waved sticklike wands, and by making patterns in the air, ~~you~~ *they* developed ~~your~~ *their* muscles.

7. Schoolbooks children used ~~they~~ were usually old and had no pictures.

8. Students had to buy ~~our~~ *their* own books, and then ~~we~~ *they* had to save them for ~~our~~ *their* younger brothers and sisters.

9. Some parents thought that girls ~~they~~ should not go to school and that ~~you~~ *they* should learn sewing and cooking at home.

10. Some doctors thought that if children spent too much time thinking in school, ~~you~~ *they* could overwork ~~your~~ *their* brains.

Next Step Describe schools today by finishing the three sentences below:

1. In newer schools, children . . .
2. In school, children exercise by . . .
3. Students have to buy . . .

Add a second sentence using at least one pronoun for each example. (Be very careful not to have any pronoun shifts or double subjects.)

Indefinite Pronouns

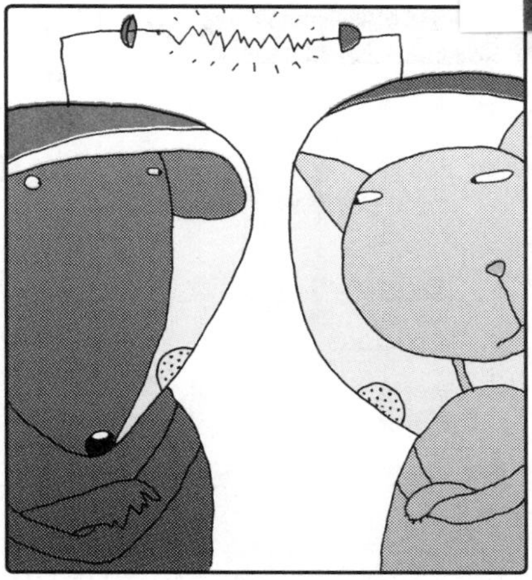

Words like *everybody, anybody,* and *everything* are **indefinite pronouns** that seem to talk about more than one person or more than one thing. They seem like plural words. But, in fact, pronouns ending in *body (everybody, somebody), thing (everything, nothing),* and *one (someone, no one)* function grammatically as singular words—as in "Everybody *has* a blank look on **her** (or **his**) face." (Turn to page 89 and section 445.2-445.3 in *Write Source 2000* for more information.)

Directions

Each of the sentences below contains an indefinite pronoun. Some of the verbs used with these pronouns are correct, and some are not. Underline each indefinite pronoun and change the verb or antecedent if necessary so that each sentence is clear and correct. The first one has been done for you.

1. Does anybody remember ~~their~~ *his (or) her* first conversation with a pet?
2. Neither the dog nor the cat wants ~~their~~ *its* ears examined.
3. Each of my friends has a pet.
4. Everything in the store's pet department ~~are~~ *is* on sale.
5. Will someone please loan me and my dog ~~their~~ *his (or) her* Frisbee?
6. Nearly half of all dogs ~~likes~~ *like* to chase after sticks and balls.
7. Has anybody lost ~~their~~ *his (or) her* box of dog treats?
8. Either my mother or my sister lost ~~their~~ *her* grooming brush.
9. Something in our cat's favorite foods is good for tartar control.
10. Most of the food in our cat's diet ~~are~~ *is* low-fat, yet tasty.
11. One of our cats ~~like~~ *likes* to sit and stare at the wall.
12. Nothing our cats do ~~surprise~~ *surprises* me any more.

Directions Use each of the following indefinite pronouns in a sentence. Underline the pronoun once and the verb twice. Be sure to use the correct singular or plural verb to go with each pronoun. The first one has been done for you. *Answers will vary.*

1. none — *None of the students in my history class are going to the parade.*
2. some ______
3. half ______
4. everyone ______
5. nothing ______
6. all ______
7. anything ______
8. nobody ______
9. one ______
10. each ______

Simple Verb Tenses

Understanding the three simple tenses, or times, of a verb is not difficult. A verb is in either the **present** tense, the **past** tense, or the **future** tense. (For more information about verb tenses, turn to 448.1 - 448.3 in *Write Source 2000*.)

EXAMPLES

Present Tense:
A present-tense verb expresses an action that is going on now or shows something that happens regularly.

People cross the country using the same routes the pioneers used.

Past Tense:
A past tense verb expresses an action that happened in the past. Many past tense verbs end in *ed*.

Pioneers crossed the country in wagon trains.

Future Tense:
A future tense verb states an action that will take place in the future. A helping verb (*will, shall, could*) helps a verb show the future tense.

You will cross the country along a pioneer route if you follow Interstate 80.

Directions **Write the past and future tenses of the following verbs:**

	Past	Future		Past	Future
1. is	was	will be	**8.** crack	cracked	will crack
2. pour	poured	will pour	**9.** move	moved	will move
3. drive	drove	will drive	**10.** travel	traveled	will travel
4. start	started	will start	**11.** swim	swam	will swim
5. eat	ate	will eat	**12.** pay	paid	will pay
6. sound	sounded	will sound	**13.** sell	sold	will sell
7. take	took	will take	**14.** fly	flew	will fly

All Write p. 385

Directions **Rewrite each sentence by changing the verb to the tenses listed. Change any other words as necessary. Keep the meaning of the new sentences as close to the original meaning as you can. The first sentences have been done for you.**

1. It was four o'clock in the morning.

   Present It is four o'clock in the morning.

   Future It will be four o'clock in the morning.

2. People poured out of every wagon and tent.

   Present People pour out of every wagon and tent.

   Future People will pour out of every wagon and tent.

3. At five o'clock, the herders will drive 5,000 oxen into the corral.

   Present The herders drive 5,000 oxen into the corral.

   Past Yesterday morning, the herders drove 5,000 oxen into the corral.

4. The drivers pick their teams and hitch them to the wagons.

   Past The drivers picked their teams and hitched them to the wagons.

   Future The drivers will pick their teams and will hitch them to the wagons.

5. At six o'clock, we will eat breakfast and load the wagons.

   Present We eat breakfast and load the wagons.

   Past Yesterday morning, we ate breakfast and loaded the wagons.

6. At seven o'clock, the 60 wagons will line up and then move out.

   Present The 60 wagons line up and then move out.

   Past Yesterday morning, the 60 wagons lined up and then moved out.

Next Step Take a short passage from a book that is written in the present tense and rewrite it in the past or future tense.

Perfect Verb Tenses

It may take some practice, but you can understand perfect verb tenses perfectly. As with simple tenses, perfect tenses deal with time. (For more information, turn to the introduction on page 448 and to 448.4-449 in *Write Source 2000*.)

EXAMPLES

Present Perfect Tense:
A present perfect verb shows action that began in the past and continues or is completed in the present.
Westerners have heard tales of lost mines.
(Add *has* or *have* to the past participle to form the present perfect tense.)

Past Perfect Tense:
A past perfect verb shows action that began and ended in the past.
Many prospectors had found and then had lost valuable mines.
(Add *had* to the past participle to form the past perfect tense.)

Future Perfect Tense:
A future perfect verb shows action that will begin and end in the future.
Mines yet to be found will have hidden their treasures for centuries.
(Add *shall have* or *will have* to the past participle to form the future perfect tense.)

Directions **List the past participles for the following present tense verbs. The first one has been done for you.**

1. be ___been___
2. tell ___told___
3. feature ___featured___
4. uncover ___uncovered___
5. find ___found___
6. kill ___killed___
7. die ___died___
8. surface ___surfaced___
9. continue ___continued___
10. scour ___scoured___
11. unearth ___unearthed___
12. fight ___fought___

All Write pp. 385 and 388-389

Directions **Use the past participles of the listed verbs with *have, had, has,* and/or *will* to form the perfect tenses as shown. The first one has been done for you.**

1. Over the years, Westerners ___have told___ *(tell)* and retold many tales of lost gold and silver mines. **(present perfect)**

2. One popular story ___has featured___ *(feature)* the legendary Lost Dutchman Mine in Arizona. **(present perfect)**

3. Along with three partners, a man known as Jake Miller ___had found___ *(find)* the mine and left a map showing its location. **(past perfect)**

4. Miller ___had killed___ *(kill)* at least three people to keep the mine a secret, and many others ___had died___ *(die)* trying to find it. **(past perfect)**

5. Many legends about the mine ___had surfaced___ *(surface)*, including one story about Apaches filling the mine with rocks. **(past perfect)**

6. People ___have continued___ *(continue)* to search for the mysterious mine and its vast treasure of gold. **(present perfect)**

7. They ___have scoured___ *(scour)* the area south of the Salt River near Weaver's Needle and the Superstition Mountains. **(present perfect)**

8. If anyone finds the Lost Dutchman or other lost mine, he or she ___will have unearthed___ *(unearth)* a long-hidden secret of the West. **(future perfect)**

9. After many years of searching, the finder of a lost mine ___will have fought___ *(fight)* against terrific odds and won. **(future perfect)**

Next Step Write out your own explanations of *present perfect, past perfect,* and *future perfect tenses.* Then compare your explanations with the ones in your handbook.

Irregular Verbs

Most verbs in the English language are said to be **regular** because they follow a simple, predictable pattern—when a regular verb goes into the past, you just add *-ed* to it. The rest of the verbs in the English language are called **irregular.** They do not follow this simple pattern. For most irregular verbs, the whole word changes in the past tense. When an irregular verb is used with *has, had,* and *have* (as a past participle), the base verb changes again. (See page 449 in *Write Source 2000* for a list of common irregular verbs.)

EXAMPLES

	Present Tense	*Past Tense*	*Past Participle*
Regular	**I talk.**	**I talked.**	**I have talked.**
Irregular	**I speak.**	**I spoke.**	**I have spoken.**

Directions **Fill in the past tense and past participle of these verbs. They are all irregular.**

	Present Tense	Past Tense	Past Participle
1.	I am happy.	I was happy.	I have been happy.
2.	He bites his lip.	He bit his lip.	He has bitten his lip.
3.	She breaks dishes.	She broke dishes.	She has broken dishes.
4.	I catch a cold.	I caught a cold.	I have caught a cold.
5.	She does yoga.	She did yoga.	She has done yoga.
6.	I drink milk.	I drank milk.	I have drunk milk.
7.	He eats pizza.	He ate pizza.	He has eaten pizza.
8.	I fall down.	I fell down.	I had fallen down.
9.	She flies a plane.	She flew a plane.	She has flown a plane.
10.	I give blood.	I gave blood.	I have given blood.

	Present Tense	Past Tense	Past Participle
11.	They go to town.	They ___went___ to town.	They have ___gone___ to town.
12.	We hide from Joe.	We ___hid___ from Joe.	We have ___hidden___ from Joe.
13.	I know the answer.	I ___knew___ the answer.	I had ___known___ the answer.
14.	She leads the band.	She ___led___ the band.	She has ___led___ the band.
15.	They ride bikes.	They ___rode___ bikes.	They have ___ridden___ bikes.
16.	I run fast.	I ___ran___ fast.	I had ___run___ fast.
17.	They see me.	They ___saw___ me.	They have ___seen___ me.
18.	We sing songs.	We ___sang___ songs.	We have ___sung___ songs.
19.	I swim swiftly.	I ___swam___ swiftly.	I have ___swum___ swiftly.
20.	I take chances.	I ___took___ chances.	I have ___taken___ chances.
21.	He throws fits.	He ___threw___ fits.	He has ___thrown___ fits.
22.	We wear hats.	We ___wore___ hats.	We have ___worn___ hats.
23.	I build models.	I ___built___ models.	I have ___built___ models.
24.	We ring the bell.	We ___rang___ the bell.	We have ___rung___ the bell.
25.	They grow apples.	They ___grew___ apples.	They have ___grown___ apples.

Next Step Find a paragraph (or two) in a book or magazine. Look at all the verbs and see if you can identify them as regular or irregular.

Transitive and Intransitive Verbs

Transitive verbs "transfer" their action to a direct object (and sometimes an indirect object). The direct object completes the meaning of the sentence, as in the examples that follow. An **intransitive** verb completes its meaning without an object. (See 450.1-450.3 in *Write Source 2000* for more information.)

EXAMPLES

Transitive Verb:

Some explorers gave kings and queens gold.

- *Direct Object:* A direct object receives the direct action of the verb. It answers the question *who?* or *what?* after the verb. Some explorers *gave* what? *(gold)*
- *Indirect Object:* An indirect object receives the action of the verb indirectly. It tells *to whom* or *for whom* something is done. Some explorers *gave* gold to whom? *(kings and queens)*

Intransitive Verb:

Some explorers gave up.

- *No Object:* An intransitive verb does not transfer its action. Its action is complete without an object.

Intransitive Verb:

Some explorers gave up before finding gold.

- *Object of a Preposition:* If an object *(gold)* follows a preposition *(before)*, it is an object of the preposition; it is not an object of the verb.

Directions **Write *T* in front of sentences with transitive verbs and *I* in front of sentences with intransitive verbs. For each transitive verb, underline the direct object and circle any indirect objects. The first one has been done for you.**

__T__ **1.** Early Egyptians sailed their boats only on the Nile River.

__I__ **2.** Ancient Egyptians thought of the world as a flat rectangle with four pillars holding up the sky.

T 3. Egyptian merchants imported ebony and ivory.

I 4. Other early explorers, such as the Phoenicians, journeyed through the Mediterranean Sea into the Atlantic Ocean to Britain.

T 5. Phoenicians sold other explorers valuables and food.

T 6. But rather than buy or trade, many explorers attacked ships and took their valuable cargo.

T 7. The Vikings stole gold, silver, and jewelry from many settlements.

I 8. Around the year 1000, Leif Ericson and his band of Vikings settled in North America at Newfoundland.

T 9. Then in 1492, in search of the East Indies Islands, Christopher Columbus discovered the West Indies and Cuba.

T 10. On the return trip, Columbus gave his officers hammocks, an idea he got from the islanders.

T 11. Columbus never told his sailors the distance they had gone because the crew was afraid of sailing off the edge of the world.

T 12. Amerigo Vespucci, the first to discover that America was a new continent, supplied other sailors maps of the New World.

Next Step Some verbs, such as *drive, read,* and *play,* can be either transitive or intransitive. Choose one of those verbs and write a sentence using it as a transitive verb, and then write another sentence using it as an intransitive verb. Afterward, see if you can think of at least 10 more verbs that can be both transitive and intransitive.

Subject-Verb Agreement 1

Subjects and verbs used together must agree in number. That is, they must both be singular or plural. In order to check for subject-verb agreement, you must first identify the main subject and its verb. Underlining the main subject once and the verb twice in your rough drafts will help you look for subject-verb agreement in your own writing. (Turn to pages 88-89 in *Write Source 2000* for help with special kinds of agreement problems.)

EXAMPLES

Rolfe studies his paint job.

(*Rolfe* is a singular subject; *studies* is a singular verb.)

For a present-tense verb to agree with a plural subject (*birds, houses, children, geese,* etc.), the verb *must not end* in *s.*

The janitors study Rolfe's painting mistake.

(*Janitors* is a plural subject; *study* is a plural present-tense verb.)

The janitors from the district office try a new paint remover.

(*Janitors,* not office, is the plural subject. *Office* is the object of the preposition *from.*)

Directions

Underline the subject once and the verb twice in the following sentences. In the space provided, identify the subject and verb as singular *S* or plural *P*. Don't be fooled by a prepositional phrase that comes between the subject and the verb. The verb must agree with the subject. The first sentence has been done for you.

S 1. The examiner tests at least 10 new drivers each day.

P 2. Most new drivers appear very nervous before their tests.

P 3. Examiners follow a checklist when testing.

S 4. An older man, during his test, stops suddenly in the middle of a road.

S 5. He then steps on the gas just as suddenly.

S 6. One nervous teenager searches frantically through his pockets for his car keys.

S 7. The examiner in the meantime examines his car.

P 8. Two happy new drivers leave the testing center with their licenses.

S 9. A middle-aged woman just misses another car in the parking lot.

S 10. She looks very nervous behind the wheel of her car.

Directions **In a paragraph, recall an exciting or important event from one of your favorite books or movies. Use the present tense when you write to help make your paragraph exciting and interesting.**

Next Step After you review your paragraph, share your work with a classmate. Check each other's work for subject-verb agreement errors.

Subject-Verb Agreement 2

It's common to find sentences in which the subjects and verbs don't agree. For example, someone might incorrectly write *The committee have adjourned* rather than *The committee has adjourned*. It's an easy mistake to make.

These activities focus on two particular problems with subject-verb agreement: sentences with collective nouns and sentences in which the subject comes after the verb. (Turn to pages 88-89 in *Write Source 2000* for explanations and examples.)

EXAMPLE

The team is preparing for its big game.

(The collective noun *team* is singular, the verb *is* is singular, and the pronoun *its* is singular. All three items are consistently singular. Make sure that collective noun-verb-pronoun combinations stay consistent.)

Directions **Underline the subject (a collective noun) for each set of verbs below; then circle the verb that agrees in number with the subject. The first one has been done for you.**

Some answers may vary.

1. The crowd in the gym (*is*, *are*) cheering loudly.
2. Measles (*has*, *have*) kept several of the best players home all week.
3. The team (*is*, *are*) required to return their jerseys after the season.
4. The pair of boots I want (*is*, *are*) in the window.
5. Mathematics (*has*, *have*) been a challenge for me.
6. The committee (*has*, *have*) voted in favor of a neighborhood party.
7. Our class (*is*, *are*) planning a square dance.
8. The faculty (*is*, *are*) asked to attend the dance.

Directions **These sentences have unusual word order. Underline the subject in each sentence below. (It will come after a helping or main verb.) Then circle the verb or helping verb that agrees with the subject. The first one has been done for you.**

1. *(Has, Have)* your brother seen that movie?
2. There on the horizon *(is, are)* the cloudlike mountain formations.
3. Beyond the small town *(was, were)* a large field of prairie-dog burrows.
4. *(Has, Have)* any of your relatives ever been to Colorado?
5. *(Wasn't, Weren't)* Bob and Sandy going to baby-sit for your brother?
6. There *(is, are)* a crowd gathering in front of the school.
7. There *(go, goes)* Sasha, followed by Andy.
8. Across the river *(are, is)* two new subdivisions.
9. Under the old buildings *(is, are)* a dark tunnel.
10. Over there *(is, are)* the paper for the project.
11. *(Is, Are)* Ellie, Meggie, or Bill going to the dance?
12. Over the river and through the woods to grandmother's house *(goes, go)* we.
13. *(Is, Are)* Blaire, Peter, and Paul taking chemistry next year?
14. There *(is, are)* many important reasons for going to school.
15. *(Do, Does)* most of America's pets eat dry food?

Next Step Explain to a partner why you decided on the answers to the 15 sentences above.

Subject-Verb Agreement 3

Sometimes it is tricky getting subjects and verbs to agree. **Compound subjects** are double trouble when it comes to agreement. When a compound subject is joined by *and,* use a plural verb. If a compound subject is connected by *or* or *nor,* use a verb that agrees with the subject closest to the verb. (For more information, turn to page 88 in *Write Source 2000.*)

EXAMPLES

Jack and Jill were on their way down the hill.
(The subject *Jack and Jill* is plural so the plural verb *were* is used.)

Neither Jack nor Jill was able to avoid falling.
(*Jill* is singular so the singular verb *was* is used.)

Jack's neighbor or his brothers were first on the scene.
(*Brothers*—the word closest to the verb—is plural so the plural verb *were* is used.)

Directions **Correct any errors in subject-verb agreement in the following sentences by changing the verbs. Do not change verbs that are correct. The first sentence has been done for you.**

1. The owner of the well and his lawyer ~~says~~ *say* Jack and Jill were trespassing.
2. Jack and Jill testify that the well and the hill ~~is~~ *are* unsafe.
3. Jack and Jill and their lawyer ~~says~~ *say* the hill should be fenced off because it is too dangerous.
4. Then one lawyer or the other ~~object~~ *objects*, and the judge pounds his gavel to quiet the courtroom.
5. Jack or Jill ~~need~~ *needs* to ask permission and to pay for each pailful of water next time he or she goes to the well.
6. Jack and Jill say to forget it; they will drink bottled water.

Subject-Verb Agreement 4

When it comes to subject-verb agreement, **indefinite pronouns** can definitely be disagreeable and confusing. Some indefinite pronouns are singular. They act as singular subjects and use singular verbs. Singular indefinite pronouns are *another, anybody, anyone, anything, each, either, everybody, everyone, everything, neither, nobody, nothing, one, somebody, someone,* and *something.*

Some indefinite pronouns can be singular or plural—it depends on the noun they refer to. When the noun in a prepositional phrase following the indefinite pronoun is singular, use a singular verb. When that noun is plural, use a plural verb. These indefinite pronouns include *all, any, most, none,* and *some.* (See page 89 in *Write Source 2000* for more information.)

EXAMPLES

Anybody who falls down a hill is in danger of being injured.

(As a subject, the singular pronoun *anybody* needs the singular verb *is.*)

Luckily, all of the water in the pail was saved.

(Since *water* is singular, the pronoun subject *all* is singular, requiring the singular verb *was.*)

All of the water bugs in the pail were not saved.

(Since *bugs* is plural, the pronoun subject *all* is plural, requiring the plural verb *were.*)

Directions **Correct any errors in subject-verb agreement in the following sentences by changing the verbs.**

1. Neither Jack's parents nor Jill's mother ~~carry~~ carries medical insurance.
2. Each of them ~~ask~~ asks the well's owner to pay the hospital bills.
3. None of the parties ~~agrees~~ agree, so they go to court.
4. According to Jack, some of the boards around the well ~~was~~ were missing.
5. "No way," says the owner. "All of that wooden platform ~~were~~ was there."
6. Everyone in the courtroom ~~start~~ starts talking to one another.
7. The jury reaches its verdict, and nobody ~~are~~ is very happy with it.
8. Half of the medical bills ~~is~~ are to be paid by the well's owner.

Identifying Verbals

Hidden in many pieces of writing are secret agents known as **verbals.** A verbal is a verb acting as another part of speech; it's a verb in disguise. **Gerunds, participles,** and **infinitives** are verbals. (For more information, see 451.1 - 451.3 in your *Write Source 2000* handbook.)

EXAMPLES

A *gerund* is a verb form ending in *-ing* that is used as a noun.

Shopping is excellent recreation.

(The noun *shopping* is the subject of this sentence.)

A *participle* is a verb form ending in *-ed* or *-ing* that is used as an adjective.

The butterfly fluttering near the daisy is a monarch.

(The adjective *fluttering* modifies "butterfly.")

An *infinitive* is a verb form introduced by the word "to" that can be used as a noun, an adjective, or an adverb.

I plan to read a book on Saturday.

(The infinitive *to read* is a noun used as a direct object.)

Directions **In the following paragraph, verbals are underlined. Above each of these words, identify what kind of verbal it is—gerund, participle, or infinitive. The first one has been done for you.**

Idalia, bored [participle] with the usual presents, asked for a pet for her birthday. Walking [gerund] a dog of her own had been her dream for a long time. A poodle puppy wagging [participle] its tail in a pet store caught her eye. Hoping [participle] for this pet, Idalia went to the store every day to look [infinitive] at the beloved pup. On her birthday, Idalia and her mom hurried to the store to buy [infinitive] the poodle. Idalia named the excited [participle] puppy Inglebert, which means "unusually intelligent." Playing [gerund] fetch and teaching [gerund] Inglebert new tricks now take up much of Idalia's time.

Directions **In the following passage, underline the verbals. Above each of these words, identify what kind of verbal it is—gerund, participle, or infinitive. The first one has been done for you.**

participle infinitive
Pausing to shake the water off her fur, the Labrador retriever
scrambled up the beach and dropped the tennis ball at her master's feet.
participle infinitive
Sighing, he picked it up to throw again. It splashed far out in the lake.
gerund
Retrieving the yellow object was all that mattered to the dog.
participle infinitive
Determined to continue the game, she bounded into the water and paddled
participle participle
to the ball. Grabbing it in her mouth and turning toward shore, she swam
participle
back as if she were in a race. Soaked but happy, she climbed out of the
water, shook again, dropped the ball, and backed expectantly for the
next throw.

He wondered how many times it would take before the dog would be
infinitive participle
too tired to swim after the ball. Feeling the warm sun on his shoulders,
infinitive
he decided that this was a good day to test her stamina. "I've got all
gerund
afternoon," he mused, "and throwing the ball is the easy part. Let's just
infinitive
see how long it takes for her to lose her enthusiasm."

Next Step On your own paper, write a paragraph about an animal. Use at least one example of each kind of verbal. Then exchange paragraphs with a classmate and circle the verbals in each other's work.

Using Specific Verbs

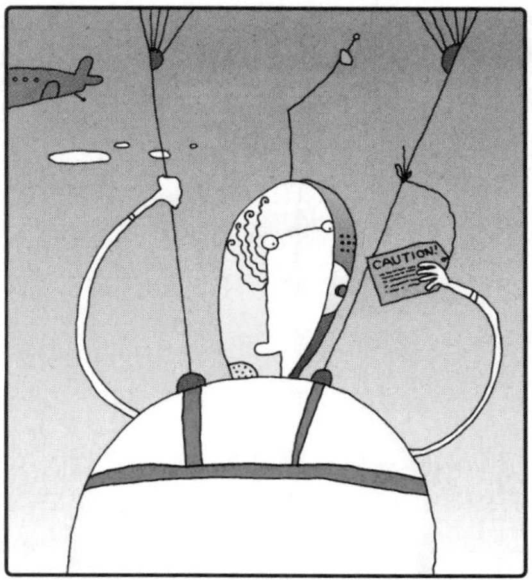

A sentence like "The plane flew past Ralphy" is too general to create an effective image or word picture. A reader can't see how the plane was flying, or how close it flew to Ralphy, or what it sounded like.

On the other hand, if the sentence were to say "The plane screamed past Ralphy," the reader would be able to see things more clearly. A specific verb like *scream* makes the sentence come alive for the reader. Specific verbs add punch to writing. (See page 135 in your *Write Source 2000* handbook.)

Directions **In each of the sentences below, substitute one vivid verb for the verb and adverb in parentheses. The first one has been done for you.**

Answers will vary.

1. Brett ____tore____ *(quickly went)* across the burning sand.
2. Donna ____examined____ *(carefully read)* the tag on her parachute.
3. Kevin ____dashed____ *(went quickly)* past the sleeping Doberman.
4. Suzy ____sprinted____ *(moved quickly)* past the other runners.
5. Miss Tinely ____shouted____ *(spoke loudly)* at her daydreaming friend.
6. Tim ____glanced____ *(looked quickly)* at the fuel gauge.
7. The white rhinoceros ____thumped____ *(walked heavily)* down the ramp.
8. The mice ____scattered____ *(moved in all directions)* to their holes.
9. The writer ____stared____ *(looked blankly)* at the unopened letter.
10. The boys ____complained____ *(talked negatively)* about the football game for half an hour.
11. Shavonne ____slurped____ *(drank noisily)* her milk shake.
12. Jesse ____nibbled____ *(ate slowly)* his hamburger.

All Write p. 92

Directions **In the paragraph below, substitute a vivid verb for each verb in parentheses.** *Answers will vary.*

I always thought it was impossible to go sledding without snow. But that was before I tried "ice blocking." Some friends and I (*got*) ____*bought*____ six 10-pound blocks of ice from a local gas station. Then we (*went*) ____*hurried*____ to a nearby park and (*took*) ____*shoved*____ the heavy blocks to the top of a large grassy hill. I (*saw*) ____*watched*____ my friends as they (*moved*) ____*barreled*____ down the steep slope; they (*sat*) ____*perched*____ carefully on towels laid on top of the blocks so they wouldn't (fall) ____*slide*____ off. Finally I (*got*) ____*mustered*____ the courage to try. Down the hill I (*moved*) ____*whizzed*____ . I hadn't realized that an ice block could (*go*) ____*shoot*____ so fast. Then, near the bottom, I (*hit*) ____*smacked into*____ a bump and (*fell*) ____*flew*____ off, rolling over and over in the grass and mud. Before long, I was (*covered*) ____*masked*____ with dirt and grime. I (*liked*) ____*enjoyed*____ "ice blocking," but sledding on snow is definitely much cleaner.

Next Step Circle five of the vivid verbs you used above. Now look up each one in a thesaurus and choose a new verb to write next to the circled one. In each one, which verb, the circled verb or the one from the thesaurus, do you like best? Why?

Adjectives

Let's say you are writing about someone whose pen suddenly popped apart during an essay test. Adjectives could help you make this action seem real for a reader. Colorful adjectives add life to writing and help you tell an effective story. However, don't overuse them; otherwise your writing will sound forced or unnatural. (For more information about choosing effective modifiers, turn to page 136 in *Write Source 2000*.)

EXAMPLE

After the *top* half of Jorge's pen rocketed across the room, the *ink* cartridge and *metal* spring followed in its path. He was left with the *useless bottom* half. (The italicized words are all adjectives. They help a reader visualize exactly what has happened.)

Directions

Beneath each of the frequently used adjectives below, list at least four colorful and creative synonyms. (Don't know what a synonym is? Look it up in your *Write Source 2000* handbook.)

nice	bad
1. ________	1. ________
2. ________	2. ________
3. ________	3. ________
4. ________	4. ________

great	old
1. ________	1. ________
2. ________	2. ________
3. ________	3. ________
4. ________	4. ________

Directions **Read and enjoy the following description of a brave, determined artist. Circle at least 20 colorful adjectives, in addition to the one already circled, in this true story.**

The Blind Seer

Our family's longtime friend Armand Merizon is more than an artist. He is a rebel, a man of vision, and something of a prophet.

When I was 13, supposedly asleep in my upstairs bedroom, his oversized personality would fill our house. He and my parents would debate for hours about politics, religion, art, and the state of the environment. His roar and his chuckle were so deep they seemed to knock the pictures crooked on the walls. In my mind, I could picture his green army coat with its bottomless pockets, his full, black beard that made him look like Fidel Castro, and his far-pointing forefinger. The blue-gray smoke from his Jamaican cigar would cloud up through the furnace vents, prick my nostrils, fill my lungs, and cling to my pajamas. I could not have known then how much of him I would take into my life.

Today he is nearly seventy and gradually going blind. Fifty years of experimentation with light and design and texture of paint on canvas are being forced to an early end. He has always filled the center of his canvases with a sparkling, brilliant light. That bright center shows the intense moment in which he sees and feels beauty. And now it is exactly the center of his vision, the bull's-eye, that he cannot see. Yet he has told me he will not stop painting until his nose touches the canvas.

He used to paint landscapes and seascapes in fine detail. He can't see the details anymore. But now he paints with fierce joy—free forms in colors that make rainbows look pale. Now you can feel his anger and hear his laughter in his abstract designs. He has always rejected society. But now, with his beard turned to gray, he loves life more than ever. And he sees it in excellent detail with his inward eye.

Using Adjectives to Compare

Special forms of adjectives are used to compare nouns. (Turn to 453.1 - 453.6 in *Write Source 2000* for more information and examples.)

EXAMPLES

Comparative Form:
I am *taller* than my brother.
(To compare two persons, places, things or ideas.)

Superlative Form:
I am the *tallest* basketball player on the team.
(To compare three or more persons, places, things or ideas.)

One-syllable, and some two-syllable, adjectives form comparatives and superlatives using *-er* and *-est* endings:
big, bigger, biggest

Most adjectives with two or more syllables form the comparative and superlative by pairing the words *more* and *most* (*less, least*) with the positive form:
terrible, more terrible, most terrible

Directions **Fill in the following blanks with the comparative and superlative forms of the adjectives given.**

	Positive	Comparative	Superlative
1.	great	greater	greatest
2.	smart	smarter	smartest
3.	caring	more caring	most caring
4.	terrific	more terrific	most terrific
5.	radiant	more radiant	most radiant
6.	weird	weirder	weirdest

Directions **Now imagine that you are a movie reviewer, and in a short paragraph, review your favorite—or least favorite—movie. Try to use a number of the adjectives (in one form or another) from the list on the previous page.**

Movie Review Paragraph

Next Step Exchange paragraphs with a classmate. Read each other's review. Then circle any comparative or superlative forms used.

Special Adjectives

There are times when you will use special adjectives in your writing. Some of these special adjectives are compound adjectives, demonstrative adjectives, indefinite adjectives, and predicate adjectives. (Turn to 452.2 - 452.5 in *Write Source 2000* for more information.)

EXAMPLES

Compound Adjectives:

A *shortleaf* pine tree has *yellow-green* needles and *scalelike* bark.

A compound adjective is made up of two or more words and is often hyphenated.

Demonstrative Adjectives:

***This* oak tree is taller than *that* pine tree.**

A demonstrative adjective helps point out a noun. *This* and *these* point out a nearby noun. *That* and *those* point out a more distant noun. (When *this, that, these,* and *those* follow nouns, they are considered pronouns and not adjectives.)

Indefinite Adjectives:

***Most* parks have *some* trees.**

An indefinite adjective gives an approximate number or quantity.

Predicate Adjectives:

The trees are *old* and *gnarled.*

A predicate adjective follows a linking verb and describes the subject.

Directions **Write a *C* above each compound adjective, a *D* above each demonstrative adjective, an *I* above each indefinite adjective, and a *P* above each predicate adjective. The first sentence has been done for you.**

Many different trees grow in North America, and wherever you live, you can see some trees. More than 600 different species of trees range across these United States. Most species are native to this continent, but a few species were brought over from several faraway places. Many trees, such as the common juniper, have widespread habitats, and some species, like the fox-tail pine, are found in just a few remote areas.

All Write p. 394

To be a tree, a plant must be tall (at least 15 feet tall) and have well-developed branches and a single woody stem. Trees have two types of leaves. Cone-bearing evergreen trees have leaves (or needles) that stay on the branches, while other trees have deciduous leaves that fall off each year. These deciduous trees include oaks, maples, and elms. Although few people would believe it, even cacti can be trees. The tree-sized saguaro is found in the Southwest, produces fruit, and has funnel-shaped flowers that have a melonlike smell. The trees that may be the most easily recognized are in the redwood family. This family includes those mighty giants, the redwood and sequoia. Many sequoias reach 12 feet in diameter and grow over 250 feet tall. These reddish-brown giants are more than 3,000 years old. Redwoods are thinner and taller than sequoias. Some have grown more than 350 feet tall. Those giant redwoods have a swampland cousin in Florida called the bald cypress. These oversized trees have scalelike bark, yellow-green needles, and round cones. A bald cypress grows to be 125 feet tall and to have a 5-foot-diameter base.

Next Step Write a list of 10 descriptive adjectives. Then see how many compound adjectives you can create by adding another word to each adjective.

Adverbs 1

As part of a unit on aeronautics, one student is testing his paper airplane design for the rest of the class. If you were to describe this scene, how could using adverbs help to make the action seem more real? By adding spice and detail to the verbs and by bringing the action into focus—that's how. See the example below. (Also, turn to 454.1-454.2 in *Write Source 2000* for more about adverbs.)

EXAMPLE

As Bryan *expertly* snapped his wrist, his sleek airplane sailed *smoothly* and *surely* above the heads of his classmates.
(*Expertly, smoothly*, and *surely* are all one-word adverbs.)

Directions **In the following sentences, locate and underline all of the one-word adverbs. The number of adverbs in each sentence is given in parentheses. The first one has been done for you. (*Note:* Do not include prepositional phrases used as adverbs.)**

1. The pilot announced, "Thunderstorms are quickly building to our left." (1)
2. John's mother hardly dared to look. (1)
3. Someone quietly said that she saw sparks suddenly flicker from one engine. (2)
4. John, a seven-year-old boy, excitedly looked around. (2)
5. Soon it was time to land in New York. (1)
6. Travelers filed quickly off the plane and hurriedly scattered everywhere. (3)
7. John and his mother searched the crowd anxiously for his aunt. (1)
8. Suddenly the airport was without any light. (1)
9. Now to move anywhere was very difficult. (3)
10. Passengers somehow found the baggage claim area in the dark. (1)

Adverbs 2

Adverbs, like adjectives, have three forms: *positive, comparative,* and *superlative.* And like adjectives, the spelling of comparative and superlative adverbs depends on the number of syllables in the positive form. (Turn to 454.1 in *Write Source 2000* for more examples.)

EXAMPLES

	One Syllable	Two or More Syllables
Positive:	**fast**	**quickly**
Comparative:	**faster**	**more quickly**
Superlative:	**fastest**	**most quickly**

Directions **Use each of the following adverbs in a sentence. Use the adverb in the form indicated in parentheses. The first one has been done for you.** *Answers will vary.*

1. firmly (comparative) *Mom gives orders more firmly than Dad.*
2. slow (superlative) ______
3. strangely (positive) ______
4. frequently (comparative) ______
5. rarely (positive) ______
6. loudly (superlative) ______

[**Next Step** Share your results with a classmate. Discuss any of your partner's sentences in which the adverbs are incorrectly formed.]

Types of Adverbs

There are four basic types of adverbs: *time, place, manner,* and *degree.* (Turn to 454.2 in *Write Source 2000* for more about adverbs.)

EXAMPLES

Time:
Terri *never* misses gymnastics.
Adverbs of time tell *when, how often,* and *how long.*

Place:
She does flips *outside* in the summer.
Adverbs of place tell *where, to where*, or *from where.*

Manner:
She warms up *gradually.*
Adverbs of manner often end in *-ly* and tell *how* something is done.

Degree:
She practices her routine *entirely* before a meet.
Adverbs of degree tell *how much* or *how little.*

Directions **In the sentences below, underline the adverbs. In front of each sentence, write *T* for time, *P* for place, *M* for manner, or *D* for degree. The first one has been done for you.**

M 1. Angel moved quickly through the lunch line.

P 2. Please step outside and clean the erasers.

T 3. The seventh graders often play softball at noon.

D 4. There is scarcely enough paper for the project.

M 5. At the spring concert, the eighth graders sang beautifully.

M 6. Tara easily won the swimming race.

T 7. The eighth graders are going on a field trip tomorrow.

P 8. Because of the rain, we won't go outside for recess.

Double Negatives

Adverbs describe the action of verbs. They also modify adjectives or other adverbs. Because they are so versatile, writers use adverbs frequently . . . and young writers often end up misusing them.

Using **double negatives** is an adverb-related problem that occurs when two negatives are used where only one is needed. Double negatives are grammatically incorrect according to the rules governing standard English. ***Note:*** Do not use *barely, hardly,* or *scarcely* with a negative word. (Turn to page 91 in *Write Source 2000.*)

EXAMPLE

Double Negative:
Mom wanted to rent a cabin, but she *doesn't* like *nothing* dirty.

Corrected:
Mom wanted to rent a cabin, but she *doesn't* like *anything* dirty.

Directions **Underline the double negatives in the following sentences. Then rewrite the sentences correctly. The first one has been done for you.** *Answers will vary.*

1. There wasn't no place without dirt.

   There wasn't any place without dirt.

2. We weren't barely through the door when we choked on dust.

   We were barely (or weren't) through the door when we choked on dust.

3. There wasn't no sign of light in the cabin, so we started washing windows.

   There was no sign of light in the cabin, so we started washing windows.

4. Mom never has no rival when it comes to cleaning.

   Mom has no rival when it comes to cleaning.

5. By afternoon, there wasn't scarcely a speck of dirt anywhere.

   By afternoon, there was scarcely (or wasn't) a speck of dirt anywhere.

6. Next year, we won't rent no cabin for a vacation; we'll take a cruise.

   Next year, we won't rent a cabin for a vacation; we'll take a cruise.

Prepositions

A **preposition** is a word that introduces a prepositional phrase. *"In the air," "over the hills," "on the ground"* are all prepositional phrases introduced by prepositions. (Turn to 455.1-455.3 in your *Write Source 2000* handbook.)

EXAMPLE

The boy *in the aviator suit* wanted to fly.
(*In the aviator suit* is a prepositional phrase starting with the preposition *in.* The phrase is used as an adjective to describe the boy. *To fly* is an infinitive—a verb with the word *to* in front of it. It is used as the direct object in the sentence.)

Directions **Underline the prepositional phrases in the following passage. (Remember prepositional phrases are used as adjectives or adverbs.) Be careful not to confuse prepositional phrases with infinitive phrases.**

Have you ever dreamed of flying—by yourself, without a plane? Well, at some time in the future, it may be more than a dream. Some day you may wake up in the morning, strap on your power pack, and fly away. Imagine jetting to school in the morning or to the park in the afternoon. Think of the time you would save, not to mention the view.

But, there are still some minor problems with the power-pack idea. Imagine what it would be like with thousands of people flying in all directions at the same time. Then there's the weather. How do you handle storms in the summer or blizzards in the winter when all you have for protection is an aviator suit? And what happens if you run short of fuel while flying?

Maybe solo flight isn't such a good idea. Now that I think about it, what's wrong with planes, trains, and automobiles?

Interjections

An **interjection** is a word or phrase used to express strong emotion or surprise. *Wow!* and *Yikes!* are two interjections. A comma or an exclamation point is usually used to separate the interjection from the rest of the sentence. (Turn to page 453 in *Write Source 2000.*)

Directions **Underline each interjection in the sentences that follow.**

1. "Good grief, Mr. Decimal, we had a test on fractions yesterday," said Al.
2. "Hallelujah!" yelled our teacher. "A test a day is good for the soul."
3. "Yeah!" blurted Clarisse. "But what about our minds?"
4. "SHSHSHSHSHSH!" hissed Mr. Decimal.
5. "Holy fractions, Mr. Decimal. If we were happy every time you gave a test, we'd be the weirdest eighth graders on earth," Clarisse explained.
6. "Hey, Clarisse, stop the wisecracks," replied Mr. Decimal patiently.
7. "Wow, Mr. Decimal," answered Clarisse, "I was just being honest."
8. "I know," explained Mr. Decimal. "But, for goodness sake, you didn't think I was being serious, did you?"
9. "Whew! That's what I was hoping!" exclaimed Clarisse.
10. "Okay, let's get back to the test."

Next Step Team up with a classmate and create a brief scene in which two or more characters express strong emotion or surprise. Consider performing this scene for your classmates.

Coordinating Conjunctions

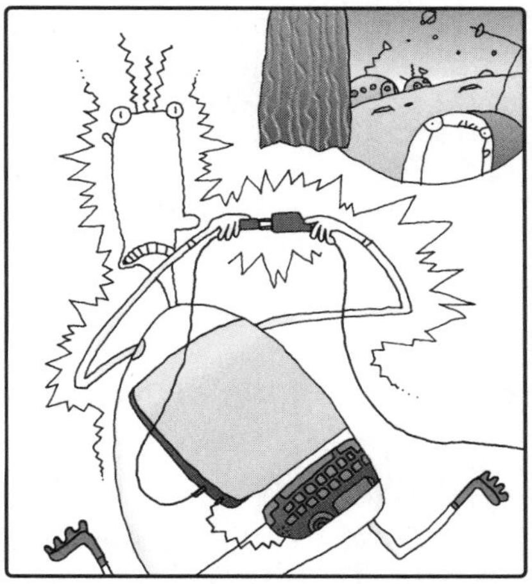

Parallel structures (two or more ideas worded in the same way) are pleasing to our "reading ear." They focus attention on certain words, add rhythm and music to sentences, and create powerful ideas.

Words, phrases, and ideas that are parallel are often connected by **coordinating conjunctions** (*and, but, so, for,* and *yet*). To make ideas parallel in your own writing, make sure that the ideas are equal and are worded in the same way. (Turn to 456.1 in *Write Source 2000* for more information.)

EXAMPLES

I hear, *and* I forget. I see, *and* I remember. I do, *and* I understand.
— Chinese proverb
(The coordinating conjunction *and* links three pairs of independent clauses.)

The book to read is not the one that thinks for you, *but* the one that makes you think.
— James McCosh
(The coordinating conjunction *but* links two dependent clauses that are worded in the same way.)

Directions **Complete each of the following sentences by adding a word, a phrase, or a clause that is parallel to the underlined portion of the sentence.** *Answers will vary.*

1. Summer can be a leisurely time for reading a good book or ________________
____.

2. When my friends and I get together for a movie marathon, we usually rent at least one horror movie, ____, and ____.

3. Packing my suitcase for our vacation is as much fun for me as ________________
____.

All Write p. 399

4. So we don't get bored on family trips, we always take along three things: paper and pencils, ____________________ , and ____________________ .

5. Labor Day signals the end of summer vacation and ____________________ ____ .

6. One day we drove all morning and saw nothing but cactus and sagebrush; then we drove all afternoon and ____________________________ .

EXAMPLE

Incorrect Sentence:
A vegetarian's diet consists of grains, plants, and the products of plants.

Correct Sentence:
A vegetarian's diet consists of grains, plants, and plant products.

Directions **Underline the idea that upsets the parallel structure in each of the following sentences. Then, on your own paper rewrite the sentence so that all the ideas are parallel.**

there are millions
1. Today there are millions of vegetarians in the United States, and Europe
of them in Europe
has millions of them, too.

2. Pythagorus, a very famous vegetarian, traveled throughout ancient Greece
life's meaning
in search of truth, knowledge, and what life means.

3. Another famous vegetarian, Sir Thomas More, was tried for high treason,
executed
found guilty, and then they executed him.

4. Vegetarians can now get special dishes at restaurants, in hospitals, and
on airplanes
vegetarian dishes are also available on airplanes.

Next Step Turn to the Preamble to the Constitution in your handbook. Read it to a partner. Then have your partner read it to you. Identify the parallel parts in this famous statement.

Correlative Conjunctions

Conjunctions join words or groups of words. **Correlative conjunctions** are conjunctions used in pairs. (For more information about correlative conjunctions, turn to 456.2 in *Write Source 2000*.)

Correlative Conjunctions:

either, or
neither, nor
not only, but also
both, and
whether, or

EXAMPLE

Both **bicycling** ***and*** **ice-skating equipment have changed over the past 100 years.**

Directions

From the list above, use a pair of correlative conjunctions to complete each sentence below. (Choose the pair of conjunctions that makes the most sense.)

1. ___Either___ baseball ___or___ football has been around since the 1870s.

2. ___Whether___ Abner Doubleday ___or___ someone else "invented" modern baseball is still being debated.

3. Before 1875, baseball catchers had ___neither___ gloves ___nor___ masks to protect themselves from a pitched ball; they stopped the ball with their chests.

4. In the first football games, players could ___both___ pick up the round football ___and___ run with it.

All Write p. 399

5. Girls were not supposed to fish or row a boat, but they could try ____either____ archery ____or____ croquet.

6. People enjoyed swimming ____whether____ it was in a pool ____or____ it was at the beach.

7. Whatever name it was known by, ____either____ badminton ____or____ poona, this sport became popular among wealthy people in the 1870s.

8. Polo was introduced from India, and it was played ____not only____ outside ____but also____ indoors.

9. ____Both____ sledding ____and____ ice-skating were popular winter sports.

10. Ice skates were made with ____either____ wooden ____or____ iron blades and had to be sharpened often.

11. Hockey requires ____not only____ strong skating skills, ____but also____ strong stick skills.

12. ____Neither____ football ____nor____ wrestling is strictly for boys anymore.

Next Step Write five sentences about a sport you enjoy. Use all five sets of correlative conjunctions listed on page 179.

Subordinating Conjunctions

A subordinating conjunction connects a dependent clause to an independent clause. (See 456.3 and 436.3 in *Write Source 2000* for more information about subordinating conjunctions.)

EXAMPLE

Subordinating Conjunction and Clause:
Fran made the team *because of her powerful serves.*

Directions **Add a dependent clause to the independent clause using the connecting subordinating conjunction that is given. The first sentence has been done for you.** *Answers will vary.*

1. The modern Olympic games began in 1896 because *a French educator thought they could make the world more peaceful.*

2. A sport often becomes more popular after ______________________________________ .

3. Some people think bowling should be an Olympic sport although ______________________________________ .

4. An Olympic gymnast makes every move look graceful as if ______________________________________ .

5. Water polo should be an Olympic sport as long as ______________________________________ .

6. Some athletes should finish their education before ______________________________________ .

All Write pp. 372 and 399

7. I could be an Olympic athlete if ______________________________

______________________________.

8. The best athletes should compete in the Olympics in order that ______________

______________________________.

9. I would love to travel to the Olympic games so ______________________

______________________________.

10. I won't be ready for the Olympics until ______________________

______________________________.

11. The Olympics should be held in my city because ______________________

______________________________.

12. I like to swim when ______________________________

______________________________.

13. Students should have no homework while ______________________

______________________________.

14. The Olympic games take place in many countries where ______________

______________________________.

15. The games are televised live unless ______________________

______________________________.

Next Step Write a paragraph telling what it would be like for you to attend or participate in the Olympic games. Include at least two sentences that use subordinate conjunctions.

Parts of Speech Review 1

Let's suppose that one day after language arts class, a stranger from a strange land asks you the following questions: What does the term **parts of speech** mean? And why do you have parts of speech? How would you answer this stranger? As a class, see if you can come up with some good answers. (For more information, turn to page 457 in your *Write Source 2000* handbook.)

Directions

Write the name of one of the eight parts of speech for each of the eight "faces." Try to name all of them on your own. Then, if the "inkwell" runs dry and you can't think of any more, refer to your handbook.

noun | verb | adjective | adverb

pronoun | preposition | interjection | conjunction

Directions **Pair up with a classmate and identify the part of speech for each underlined word. There are five examples of each part of speech, except for the interjection, which has one example.**

At *[preposition]* the beginning of last *[adjective]* year, a new girl joined our class *[noun]*. Her name was Kim, but everyone *[pronoun]* called *[verb]* her "Bigfoot" because of the size of her feet. Some kids occasionally *[adverb]* teased her, not just because she was new, but *[conjunction]* because she was different. She looked as if she were *[verb]* two grades older than we were. Kim was tall and would always *[adverb]* look at her feet when she walked. Maybe she was afraid she was going to run them into something.

Since *[Conjunction]* my parents knew her parents *[noun]* from church, they pushed *[verb]* me to be nice to her *[pronoun]*, to stick up for her, and to hang around with *[preposition]* her. I wasn't thrilled, but Kim turned out to be pretty nice. She helped me with *[preposition]* my math homework *[noun]*. She also made some pretty funny *[adjective]* remarks *[noun]* about *[preposition]* Mr. Wheeler, the gym *[adjective]* teacher, when *[conjunction]* he was out of earshot. One day Kim taped his whistle to his clipboard. It wasn't until he *[pronoun]* went to reach for it to whistle at Clyde, who was bouncing *[verb]* a basketball repeatedly *[adverb]* off Mike, that he noticed what Kim had done. We both laughed so loudly *[adverb]* that he knew we were guilty. We *[pronoun]* got a week's detention for *[preposition]* that stunt.

Kim doesn't pull crazy *[adjective]* stunts like that anymore. And nobody ever *[adverb]* makes *[verb]* fun of her or *[conjunction]* calls her "Bigfoot" either. She's a good *[adjective]* friend *[noun]* and *[conjunction]* a nice person. Gee *[interjection]*, she should have let us *[pronoun]* know right from the start.

Parts of Speech Review 2

When you write, some words can be used in many different ways. For example, a particular word in one sentence may be a noun and then in the next sentence an adjective. Knowing the eight parts of speech will help you to understand how a word can be used in a sentence. The eight parts of speech include adjectives, adverbs, conjunctions, interjections, nouns, prepositions, pronouns, and verbs. (See the sample sentences below in which the word *dog* is used as four different parts of speech. Turn to page 457 in your *Write Source 2000* handbook for more information.)

EXAMPLES

The *dog* barked to get some more *dog* food.
(noun) (adjective)

The runner was *dogging* it because he was *dog* tired.
(verb) (adverb)

Directions **Review the parts of speech in your handbook. Then label the part of speech for each underlined word in this excerpt from a speech by George Graham Vest. He was a United States senator from Missouri from 1879 to 1903. He made this speech while he was a lawyer representing a man whose dog was killed. Vest's speech helped him win the case.**

The best (adjective) friend a man has in the world may turn against (preposition) him and become his enemy. His son or daughter whom (pronoun) he has reared with loving care (noun) may (verb) prove ungrateful. The money that a man has, he (pronoun) may lose. It flies away from him, perhaps when (conjunction) he needs it most. A man's reputation may be sacrificed (verb) in a moment of ill-considered (adjective) action. The one absolutely (adverb) unselfish friend that a man can have in this selfish (adjective) world, the one that never (adverb) deserts him, the one (pronoun) that never proves ungrateful or (conjunction) treacherous is his dog. Yes (interjection), a man's dog stands (verb) by him in prosperity and in poverty (noun), in health and in sickness. He will sleep <u>on</u> (preposition) the cold ground, where the <u>wintry</u> (adjective) winds blow and the snow drives <u>fiercely</u> (adverb), if only he may be <u>near</u> (preposition) his master's side. When all other friends desert, he remains. <u>Oh</u> (interjection), when riches take wings, and <u>reputation</u> (noun) falls to pieces, he is as constant in his love as the sun in <u>its</u> (pronoun) journey <u>through</u> (preposition) the heavens. <u>And</u> (conjunction) when the last scene of all comes, and death takes his master, no matter if all other <u>friends</u> (noun) pursue their way, there by the graveside will the noble dog <u>be</u> (verb) found, his head between his paws, his eyes sad, <u>but</u> (conjunction) open in alert watchfulness, <u>faithful</u> (adjective) and true even in death.

Directions **Pick one of the following words and use it in several sentences as at least three different parts of speech. Then pick another word and try again.**

Words: **ape, back, run, green, hand, light, like, out, small, stop**

____

____

____

____

____

____

____

Next Step Wow, write a sentence and happily use all eight parts of speech in it (just like this one). Then work together with a classmate and write three sentences that include all eight parts of speech in each sentence. See if you can write one using 10 or fewer words!